Devotions & More for Girls

Ages 6–9

God
and
Me 3

LEGACY PRESS®

www.legacyXpress.com

Devotions & More for Girls

God and Me 3

Ages 6-9

By Kathy Widenhouse

DEDICATION: To my faithful prayer partners Cindy Frye and Nancy Pennington who interceded for this book from start to finish.

GOD AND ME! 3 FOR AGES 6-9

©2010 by Legacy Press, second printing
ISBN 10: 1-58411-092-9
ISBN 13: 978-1-58411-092-7
Legacy reorder #LP46835
JUVENILE NONFICTION / Religion / Devotion & Prayer

Legacy Press
P.O. Box 261129
San Diego, CA 92196
www.legacyXpress.com

Mixed Sources
Product group from well-managed
forests and other controlled sources
www.fsc.org Cert no. SGS-COC-004441
© 1996 Forest Stewardship Council

Cover and Interior Illustrator: Dave Carleson

Unless otherwise noted, Scriptures are from the *Holy Bible: New International Version* (North American Edition), copyright ©1973, 1978, 1984 by the International Bible Society. Used by permission of Zondervan Bible Publishers.

Printed in South Korea

Table of Contents

Table of Contents

Introduction

You can be close to God! Think about it: God made every single person in the entire world. He knows everything that's going on with everybody. And He wants to be your extra-special, super-close Friend!

Being close to God is different from being close to a girlfriend you see sitting next to you in a chair. You learn to be friends with God by "seeing" Him and "knowing" Him in your heart and mind.

Even Jesus' disciples had to learn this different way of being friends. Jesus showed them how to talk with God, how to listen to God, and how to do what God says. He taught them a special prayer, called "The Lord's Prayer," to help them. You can learn The Lord's Prayer and how to be close friends with God, too!

The devotions in *God & Me! 3* are built around the special lessons Jesus taught His friends. You can read them with your parents, with a friend, or on your own. You can read them in any order.

How to Use God and Me 3!

1. **Read** the title, the Bible verse, and the story. Try to understand how they fit together.

2. **Answer** the questions. Use them to help figure out what the story means to you.

3. **Pray** to God. Ask Him to help you use what you just learned. Take a minute to listen for God's voice in your heart and mind.

4. **Complete** the activity to help you act on what you just learned. You'll find answers to the puzzles at the back of the book.

Being friends with God is awesome! Don't wait any longer. Have fun learning how to be God's extra-special, super-close friend as you read *God & Me 3!*

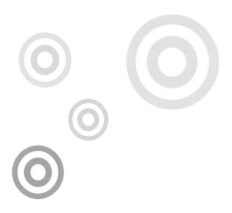

I talk to God and God talks to me.

This, then, is how you should pray:
Our Father in heaven,
hallowed be your name,

your kingdom come,
your will be done
on earth as it is in heaven.

Give us today our daily bread.

Forgive us our debts,
as we also have forgiven our debtors.

And lead us not into temptation,
but deliver us from the evil one.

~ Matthew 6:9-13

God is My Friend

I Can Talk to God

Friends talk with each other and listen to each other.

I have called you friends, for everything that I learned from my Father I have made known to you.

~ John 15:15

A Good Friend

Beth liked talking with Mr. Browne, the music teacher. He'd heard her singing in music class and told her that she had a good voice.

One day, Beth noticed that Mr. Browne wore an ankle cast. "I'm sorry you hurt your ankle," she said. "What happened?" She listened as he explained how he'd tripped on the stairs.

"Thank you, Beth, for asking about my ankle," he said. "You're a good friend. You talk and listen."

A good friend. Beth smiled. She liked that.

Beth learned something very important: friends talk with each other and listen to each other.

Jesus talked to His disciples about God and told them everything He could. He also listened to them. He was a good friend to His disciples.

You can talk to Jesus when you pray; He'll always listen. Jesus will talk to you, too. He'll tell you everything He can about God. You can listen to Jesus in your heart and when you read the Bible. He's your Friend.

Your Turn

1. List some friends that you can talk to and who will listen back.
2. Good friends talk about things that are on their minds. Name one thing that you'd like to talk about with a good friend right now.

_____

_____

_____

_____

Prayer

Jesus, I'm so glad I can talk to You and that You listen back to me. Right now, I want to talk to You about (name what's on your mind right now). Thank You for listening. Amen.

Talk and Listen to Jesus

You can talk and listen to Jesus. Draw a picture of yourself next to Him!

I Can Pray Like Jesus

Jesus teaches me how to talk with God.

This, then, is how you should pray.

~ Matthew 6:9

Jesus' Special Prayer

It was Ginny's favorite time in the worship service. The whole church became quiet. All the people bowed their heads. Then, the entire congregation said a prayer together. Everyone knew the words. Ginny wanted to join in, but she didn't know how.

"Can you teach me that prayer, Dad?" she whispered to her father. He nodded. Ginny wanted to know how to talk to God. She was ready to get closer to Him.

When Jesus lived on earth, His friends asked Him the same thing. They saw that Jesus talked with God. They wanted to know how to be close to God, too. They were ready to learn.

Jesus explained that they could talk to God. Then He showed them how. The prayer He taught them is called "The Lord's Prayer."

Jesus' special prayer is an example we can follow. You can find it in Matthew 6:9-13. As you learn the words, think about them and act on them in your life, Jesus' special prayer will help you get closer to God!

Your Turn

1. Do the members of your church say Jesus' special prayer together?
2. How can having the example of Jesus' prayer help you learn how to pray?

_____

_____

_____

_____

Prayer

Lord, teach me to pray. I want to learn. Amen.

Prayer Bookmark

Make this bookmark to remind you about Jesus' prayer example.

What you need:
1. Construction paper or card stock
2. Ruler
3. Pencil
4. Scissors
5. Markers

What to do:

Measure and then cut a piece of construction paper or card stock, 2 inches wide by 8 inches long. Use markers to write, "Lord, teach me to pray!" on the bookmark. Use markers to decorate the bookmark with a border, hearts and any other designs you prefer. With scissors, fringe the bottom edge of the bookmark.

Use your Prayer Bookmark to keep your place in *God & Me! 3* as you read these devotions.

I Can Pray with Others

I can learn how to pray by praying with others.

One of his disciples said to him, "Lord, teach us to pray."

~ Luke 11:1

Hannah's Prayer

Hannah sat in the pew looking up at Pastor Sullivan. She liked listening to him pray; his voice was warm and gentle. But now he said something that got her attention. "Will you pray along with me?" he said.

Hannah bowed her head and listened along with the prayer. She thought about God. She thanked Him for loving her. Pastor Sullivan stopped praying for a few minutes so that people could tell God they were sorry for their mistakes. Hannah thought about how she had yelled at her brother just that morning.

The pastor started praying again. Hannah asked God to help the people that the pastor named.

When the prayer was over, Hannah felt cleaner on the inside. She leaned over to her mother. "I prayed along with Pastor Sullivan," she whispered. "I think I can pray that way at home on my own, don't you?" Her mother smiled, nodded and squeezed her hand.

God puts people in our lives to help us learn to get close to Him. One way you can learn to pray is by praying along with other people!

Your Turn

1. How did Pastor Sullivan's prayer help Hannah?
2. Hannah did her part to learn how to pray. What did she do?

_____

_____

_____

_____

_____

Prayer

Dear Lord, thank You for the people You put in my life that can help teach me how to pray. Amen.

Prayer Partners

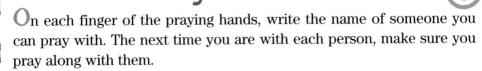

On each finger of the praying hands, write the name of someone you can pray with. The next time you are with each person, make sure you pray along with them.

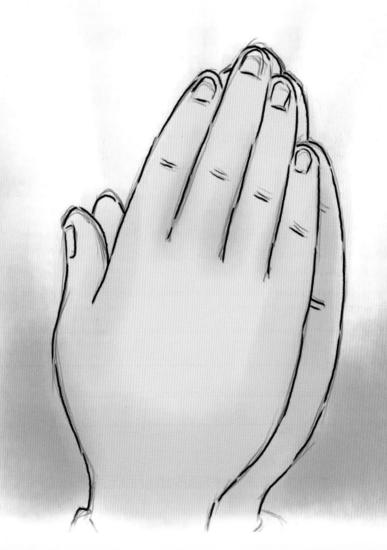

I Can Be Myself with God

I can be myself when I talk with God.

The things that come out of the mouth come from the heart.
~ Matthew 15:18

A Simple Prayer

Pastor Andrews was new to Sydney's church. He'd been with them for just three weeks.

"I like how he uses simple words in his prayers," said Sydney's mom. "He talks to God using 'You,' rather than 'Thee' or 'Thou.'"

Sydney's dad agreed. "He is sincere. Pastor Andrews doesn't puff up his prayers with extra words. Instead, he's himself—he talks with God from his heart."

Sydney thought about what her parents said. It made sense. She never heard anyone use "Thee" or "Thou" when they were talking to each other in regular conversations.

"Maybe people are afraid to be themselves," said Sydney. "They think they can fool God."

"I think you're on to something there, Sydney," said her dad. "Pastor Andrews doesn't try to kid anybody."

God already knows what you think and He loves you just as you are. Be yourself when you talk to God!

Your Turn

1. Do you ever feel tempted to use fancy words when you pray?
2. Have you ever thought you could fool God by praying what you thought He wanted to hear?
3. How do your prayers show what's going on in your heart?

_____

_____

_____

Prayer

Lord, I can't fool you. You know my heart. Help me to be myself when I talk with You. Amen.

Prayers That Don't Kid

W hat kind of prayer doesn't kid around? Cross out all the X's. Write out the remaining letters on the spaces to find out what's the honest way to pray. *Puzzle solutions appear at the back of the book.*

X F X R X O X M   X T X H X E

_ _ _ _ _   _ _ _

X H X E A X R X T

_ _ _ _ _

I Can Count on God to Listen

God listens to me when I pray.

*You will call upon me and come and pray to me,
and I will listen to you.*

~ Jeremiah 29:12

Lakisha's Weekend with Dad

Lakisha's parents were divorced. Her father promised that she could spend the weekends with him and she always looked forward to seeing him. One Friday, she had her overnight backpack ready, but her dad called that afternoon and said he had to go away on a business trip. He was sad because he wanted to see Lakisha, and he knew he let her down. Lakisha's father wanted to keep his promise, but he couldn't.

Lots of times, people are true to their word. But sometimes, even when people plan their best and try their hardest to do what they've promised, they find they can't.

This is one way that God is different from people. He has a special ability to always do what He promises. That's why God's promise about listening is so special. He says that anytime you pray, He will listen. Nothing will get in His way.

You can count on God listening to you when you pray! That's a promise. He'll keep it.

Your Turn

1. Have you ever had a friend make a promise and then not keep it?
2. Why is God able to keep all His promises?
3. Why does God's promise to listen show that He's your friend?

_____

_____

_____

Prayer

Lord, thank You that you keep Your promise to listen to me. I'm glad you are my friend. Amen.

He'll Listen All the Time

God promises to listen to you anytime, anywhere. List different places you go during your day. Use your list to help you remember to talk to Him at different times and places today!

God listens to me when...

I'm Always Near God

God is always near me.

The LORD is near to all who call on him.

~ Psalm 145:18

Rosa's Bad Dream

Rosa's family had just moved into their new house. One afternoon, the neighbor's dog barged in through the front door, growling at Rosa and baring his teeth. Rosa ran to the end of the hallway. The dog snapped at her heels. "Daddy!" she screamed. "Help! The dog is trying to hurt me!"

Rosa felt strong arms around her. She blinked, looked up and saw that she wasn't in the hallway at all. Instead, she was snuggled safely in her bed in her new bedroom. Her father sat next to her with a reassuring smile on his face. The dog was nowhere in sight.

"You had a bad dream," explained Rosa's father. "It was easy for me to hear you call out in our new house because my room is right across the hallway."

Rosa felt calmer. "It's good to know you're so close!" she said. "I'm glad my bedroom isn't in the basement."

Rosa's father heard her because he was nearby. God is near to you no matter where you are, even if you're in a new town, a new house… or even if you're in the basement!

Your Turn

1. How does it feel to call out and have someone answer?
2. Why would God want you to know that He is always near you?

_____

_____

_____

_____

_____

_____

Prayer

God, I'm so thankful that You are near to me whenever I call out to You. Amen.

A Special Place

Draw a picture of yourself in an unusual place in your house. Then go to that special place, call out to God, and thank Him for being near to you there!

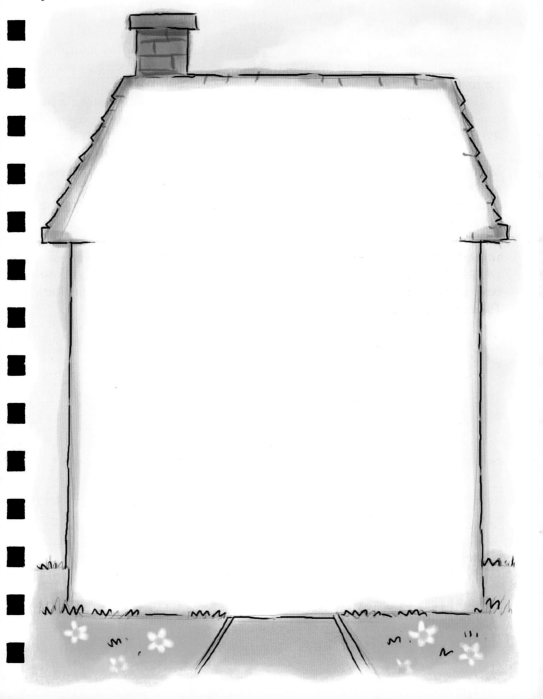

I Can Call God Anytime

God answers me when I call.
Call to me and I will answer you.
~ Jeremiah 33:3

Danielle Leaves a Message

Danielle looked outside. It was a rainy, dreary Saturday morning. "Would you like to call Angie to see if she can come over today to play?" Danielle's mother asked.

Danielle nodded eagerly. She reached for the family phone book, found Angie's number and dialed. The phone rang one … two … three … four … five times. Then Danielle heard a voice! Was it Angie?

"We can't come to the phone right now. Please leave a message after the tone and we'll return your call," the recording on the answering machine announced. Beep. Danielle spoke clearly into the phone, giving her name and number so Angie could call her back, but she hung up in disappointment. Angie was not there.

When you telephone a friend, you may get to talk with her. Or, like Danielle, you may have to leave a message and wait. But God never asks you to leave a message. That's why Jeremiah 33:3 is called "God's Telephone Number." That verse gives this wonderful promise: God always answers when you call to Him!

Your Turn

1. Why did Danielle feel disappointed?
2. Have you ever been disappointed when a friend didn't answer the phone? When?
3. Why is God's promise in Jeremiah 33:3 so special?

_____

_____

_____

Prayer

Dear God, thank You for always being there, always listening and always answering me when I call. Amen.

My Telephone Book

Fill in the phone numbers of your family and friends. Be sure to write down God's number first!

I Can Listen to God

I can listen for God's nudge to pray.

Pray in the Spirit on all occasions with all kinds of prayers and requests.

~ Ephesians 6:18

Jessie Hears From God

There were a lot of customers in the bank. Five tellers helped people, one by one. Jessie and her mother waited in line for their turn.

Jessie saw another family enter the bank. The father pushed a young girl in a wheelchair. Both her legs were in casts and her eyes were sad. The mother walked alongside them.

Jessie looked down at her sneakers. She thought about the fun she had yesterday playing soccer. She thought about what it would be like not to be able to swim. In her mind and in her heart, Jessie felt a nudge to pray.

Very quickly and quietly, Jessie talked to God. *Thank You for my legs. Thank You that they work. Please, God, help the girl in the wheelchair be healthy and happy.*

Try to listen for God's nudges during the day. Then, take a minute and talk to Him, no matter where you are … even if you're in the bank!

Your Turn

1. Do you think Jessie expected God to nudge her in the bank? Why or why not?
2. Have you ever felt a nudge from God in an unusual place or at an unusual time?
3. Sometimes we miss God's nudges because we're not listening for them. What can you do to keep your ears open to God during the day?

_____

_____

_____

_____

_____

Prayer

Lord, I'm listening for Your nudge today. Help me hear You and then pray. Amen.

Nudges in My Day

Name a nudge you might hear from God at these different times during your day.

I Can Keep Praying

Prayer takes practice.

Jesus told his disciples a parable to show them that they should always pray and not give up.

~ Luke 18:1

Kristen Keeps Trying

Kristen wanted to get an A in math. She was discouraged when she got a poor mark on a quiz. Adding, subtracting, multiplying and dividing were not easy for her. But instead of giving up, Kristen spent extra time on her homework. At the end of the semester, she looked at her report card: Next to math there was an A!

Sierra didn't score a single point during her first basketball game. She wanted to be a better basketball player, so she didn't give up. Every day after school, Sierra dribbled her basketball up and down the driveway. She shot hundreds of baskets. She practiced her free throws. During the last game of the season, she set a personal best record for baskets!

Like math for Kristen and basketball for Sierra, getting better at prayer takes practice. When you're learning to pray, it can be easy for you to give up.

Jesus understands. He wants you to keep trying. That's why He told the story of a widow who didn't give up.

Don't get discouraged when you're learning to get close to God. A lot of people stop trying. It takes more effort to try over and over like the widow. Jesus told her story so you would know you're not alone. Prayer takes practice. Keep on praying and don't give up!

Your Turn

1. Do you ever get discouraged about learning to get close to God?
2. What can happen when you get discouraged about prayer?
3. Prayer takes practice. How does Jesus' story about the widow encourage you to keep praying?

_____

_____

_____

Prayer

Lord, I want to know You and be close to You. Help me to always pray and not give up. Amen.

One Way to Practice Praying

Solve this puzzle to find one way you can practice praying. Replace each number with the letters in the key. *Puzzle solutions appear at the back of the book.*

```
          7   8   1   11

         ___ ___ ___ ___

 2   6   5   9   3   5   10   1   4   4   11

___ ___ ___ ___ ___ ___ ___ ___ ___ ___ ___
```

(1 Thessalonians 5:17)

```
 1   2   3   4   5   6   7   8   9   10   11
 A   C   I   L   N   O   P   R   T   U    Y
```

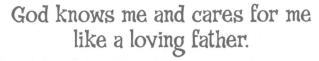

God knows me and cares for me like a loving father.

This, then, is how you should pray:
Our Father in heaven,
hallowed be your name,

your kingdom come,
your will be done
on earth as it is in heaven.

Give us today our daily bread.

Forgive us our debts,
as we also have forgiven our debtors.

And lead us not into temptation,
but deliver us from the evil one.

~ Matthew 6:9-13

God is My Heavenly Father

God Calls Himself "Father"

God shows me fatherly love.

*I will be a Father to you, and you will be
my sons and daughters, says the Lord Almighty.*

~ 2 Corinthians 6:18

A Father's Love

There's a song called, "You are My Sunshine." The words are,

> You are my sunshine
> My only sunshine
> You make me happy
> When skies are gray.

The singer uses those words to explain how she sees a special person in her life—someone who makes her happy, even when she's sad. The words compare her special person to sunshine. Sunshine is bright and cheerful. The comparison helps people understand how the singer feels.

God knows that it can be hard for you to understand Him. But He knows that you understand what a father's love can be like. Fathers give life to their children. They care for their children and protect them.

God wants you to understand His love for you, so He compares Himself to a father. A father's love is an idea that's familiar to you. Like a good father, God gives you life, cares for you, and protects you. That's why He calls Himself your heavenly Father.

Your Turn

1. Why does God compare Himself to a father?
2. List some ways God shows you fatherly love.

_____

_____

_____

_____

_____

Prayer

Father God, I love You. Thank You for giving me life, caring for me and protecting me. Amen.

God's Fatherly Love

How does God show love like a father? Write down your answer inside the sun.

God Planned for You

My heavenly Father gave me life.
You gave me life.

~ Job 10:12

Becca's Home Video

Becca and her family watched home videos from when she was a baby. "Look, Becca," said her younger brother, Joey. "Your face is red and wrinkled."

Becca giggled. She saw the baby on the screen open its mouth and yawn. A nurse handed the baby to a pretty young woman—her mother. The video picture shook.

"Dad, were you filming this?" Becca asked. "It's out of focus." She looked at her father. He ran a hand over his eyes, wiping them.

"Yes, Becca," her dad answered quietly as Becca's mother reached over and touched his hand. "The film is out of focus because I got choked up when you were born. And I still do when I think of how much you and Joey mean to me. I'm so happy I could help bring you into the world."

Your earthly father played an important part in your birth. Your heavenly Father did even more! He's the One who planned for you to be a person. He made sure you were born because He loves you so much. He planned carefully for that special day to happen!

Your Turn

1. What do Becca and her brother mean to their earthly dad?
2. God is your heavenly Father. You are His child. Below, write down what you think you mean to Him.

_____

_____

_____

_____

_____

Prayer

Father, thank You for planning for me to be born and for giving me life. Amen.

Heavenly Father's Day Planner

God planned for you to be born. Fill in the blanks to record what He considered on that special day. Have your parents help you.

To Be Born:_____
(your name)

Date:_____
(your birthdate)

Time:_____
(your time of birth)

Place:_____
(where you were born)

Weather:_____
(conditions on that day)

Other Events:_____

(other events in your family, community, nation, and world going on that day)

God's Big, Big Love

God cares for me with a father's deep, sincere love.
Consider the great love of the LORD.
~ Psalm 107:43

How Much Do You Love Me?

Sharise and her father played a special game every night when they prayed together at bedtime. "How much do you love me, Daddy?" she always asked. "Do you love me this much?" Sharise pressed together her thumb and index finger, and then opened them a little bit.

"No, I love you much more than that!" Sharise's dad always answered, smiling. "I love you this much!" He spread his arms as wide as he could.

God's fatherly love for you is even bigger! In fact, the Bible says it's hard for us to imagine "how wide and long and high and deep is the love of Christ" (Ephesians 3:18).

God's love for you is bigger, greater, wider, longer, higher, and deeper than any other love! He wants you to feel His big, big love so you can be close to Him, know Him better, and walk with Him every day.

Your Turn

1. Why does God want you to know that He loves you so much?
2. Why is it important that you feel God's big, big love?

_____

_____

_____

_____

_____

_____

_____

Prayer

Heavenly Father, thank You for Your big, big love. I love you back. Amen.

How Big is God's Love?

God planned long ago to spend time with you now. God's invitation to you is found in the Bible. Fill in the blanks below to see how much God loves you.

Wider than _____

(name the largest field or park you know)

Longer than _____

(name the longest road or street you know)

Higher than _____

(name the highest building or mountain you know)

Deeper than _____

(name the deepest river or lake you know)

God Cares

God cares for me.
*Cast all your anxiety on him
because he cares for you.*

~ 1 Peter 5:7

Maya Falls Down

The students rushed inside from the playground during the sudden rain storm. The school halls were crowded and the floors were wet. In the confusion, Maya slipped and fell, cutting her knee.

Maya was afraid. Other students just kept walking by. She covered her face with her hands. Did anyone care that she was hurt?

Maya felt a hand on her shoulder. It was Mrs. Wilson, the school nurse. "Maya, I just saw you fall down," she said. "Are you hurt? It looks like you may need a bandage." Maya felt better. Mrs. Wilson saw her accident. The nurse cared about her!

It's easy to think no one sees or cares when you have a problem. Maya felt alone until she realized Mrs. Wilson was there and saw everything that happened.

Don't believe that you're alone. Look up and look to your heavenly Father. He sees everything. He cares for you.

Your Turn

1. Name a time when you've felt all alone.
2. Write down what you can do to feel close to God when you have a problem.

_____

_____

_____

_____

_____

Prayer

Father God, I know I'm never alone. You love me and You care about me. Remind me to look up to You for help. Amen.

Care-4-U Bandage

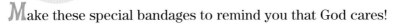

Make these special bandages to remind you that God cares!

What you need:

1. Solid color self-adhesive bandages
2. Fabric paint pens or markers
3. Paper plate

What to do:

Lay a bandage on the paper plate. Use a pen or a marker to write "God Cares" on the bandage. Add other designs as you like. Allow the ink to dry completely.

Keep the bandage in a safe place. Use it when you are hurt to remind you that God cares for you!

God is Powerful

My heavenly Father is powerful.

*All the peoples of the earth might know
that the hand of the LORD is powerful.*

~ Joshua 4:24

Abby Uses Her Hands

Abby's hands buttoned up her baby sister's ski jacket. With her hands, she lifted up her backpack and put it on her back. She reached out her hands to grab the rail and steady herself as she walked down the stairs from the porch to the driveway.

You use your hands for nearly everything. They are very important. That's why in the Bible, God compares His power to His hands.

Abby used her hands to help. Her hands gave her the strength to lift things and her hands steadied her.

In the same way, God's power helps you, strengthens you and steadies you. His hands are strong. He has hands of power.

Your Turn

1. Name things you do with your hands.
2. Why does God compare His power to hands?
3. How are your hands and God's hands (God's power) different?

_____

_____

_____

_____

_____

_____

Prayer

Heavenly Father, Your hands help me, strengthen me and steady me. You have hands of power. Amen.

God's Hands of Power

Read how God compares His hands to His power. Draw a line from each picture to the Bible verse that fits best. *Puzzle solutions appear at the back of the book.*

Because he is at my right hand, I will not be shaken.
~ *Psalm 16:8*

You save by your right hand.
~ *Psalm 17:7*

Help us with your right hand.
~ *Psalm 60:5*

God is My Shield

My heavenly Father protects me.
The LORD is my strength and my shield;
my heart trusts in him, and I am helped.
~ Psalm 28:7

The Big Storm

"It's going to rain!" Tiffany's dad called. But Tiffany raced Jeremy to the tallest slide anyway. She saw the sky get dark, but that didn't matter. She was having too much fun with the kids at the playground during the home school group picnic.

Jeremy reached the slide before Tiffany. He scrambled to the top. Tiffany looked up as Jeremy slid down. *Crack!* A jagged lightning bolt lit up the sky. *Boom!* Tiffany covered her ears. Thunder scared her.

"Help!" Tiffany cried out. Dad had warned her about the storm. She needed him now. Tiffany turned to look towards the picnic clubhouse. She couldn't see anyone. Her body shook from the gusts of wind. She covered her face so that playground sand wouldn't get in her eyes.

Strong arms wrapped around Tiffany, shielding her. It was her father! "I'm so glad you came to get me," she said. She looked over at Jeremy. His father was helping him, too.

"Come on," said Tiffany's dad. "I'll get you to the clubhouse. You're safe."

Just like Tiffany's dad, your heavenly Father protects you. He gives you ways to make good decisions so you can be safe. He can be your Shield when you're in a bad situation and when you call out for His help.

Your Turn

1. How did Tiffany's dad help protect her?
2. How does God protect you?

_____

_____

_____

Prayer

Lord, You are my Protector and my Shield. Remind me to pay attention when You warn me about danger. Show me how to turn to You for protection. Amen.

My God Shield

Connect the dots to see one way God protects you. *Puzzle solutions appear at the back of the book.*

God Knows Me

I belong to my heavenly Father and He understands me.

The Lord knows those who are his.

~ 2 Timothy 2:19

Alexis Tries to Help

Victoria's brother was very sick. He was in the hospital and the doctors didn't know if her brother would get better or not.

Victoria told her friend Alexis about her brother. "I know how you feel," said Alexis. "My sister had her appendix burst. She had to have an operation. But she got better."

Victoria turned away. Alexis tried to help. But Alexis couldn't understand exactly how Victoria felt—alone and afraid. Her brother's future was uncertain.

Alexis saw that Victoria was disappointed. "Victoria," she said, running over to hug her friend. "I can't understand exactly how you feel. My sister is different from your brother." She paused. "I'm sorry your brother is sick. It's hard."

Alexis was right. She couldn't understand Victoria's situation exactly. People can know a little bit about how you feel, and they can show they care. But you are different from anyone else. Your thoughts and feelings are one-of-a-kind.

God knows. God understands your exact feelings. He knows your thoughts and your heart. You're never alone when you know your heavenly Father and His love for You!

Your Turn

1. Describe a time you told someone how you felt and they didn't understand.
2. What can you do to remember to turn to God when you feel alone?

_____

_____

_____

Prayer

God, I'm Your girl! I'm so glad that You know me. Help me to tell You how I feel and what I think, especially when I feel no one understands. Amen.

My One-of-a-Kind Thoughts

Write down some one-of-a-kind thoughts you have that only God can understand. Pray them back to God.

God is My Heavenly Daddy

My heavenly father is close to me, like a daddy.
God sent the Spirit of his Son into our hearts,
the Spirit who calls out, "Abba, Father."

~ Galatians 4:6

Kelsey Visits Daddy

Kelsey was close to her father even though he lived in a different state. She talked with him every day on the phone. He came to see her every few weeks. She felt good whenever she was near him. Now she was visiting him for two weeks. "Daddy!" she shouted as she got off the airplane and ran into his arms.

"Daddy" is a special name Kelsey used for her father because she was close to him. Jesus was close to His Father. He had a special name for Him, too. It is "Abba."

Jesus' name for God may seem unusual to you. It's an Aramaic *(air-uh-may-ick)* word. Aramaic is the language Jesus spoke when He lived on earth.

You can speak Aramaic, like Jesus, when you talk to God. You can use Jesus' special name for God. Call Him "Abba." He's your heavenly Daddy!

Your Turn

1. What do you call your earthly father (or guardian)?
2. Why is the name "Abba" so special?

_____

_____

_____

_____

_____

Prayer

Abba, thank You for being my heavenly Daddy. Let me stay close to you. Amen.

God is My Abba

Color the poster to remind you that God is your heavenly daddy.

God is the Best

My heavenly Father is greater than anyone or anything.
My Father ... is greater than all.
~ John 10:29

The Best Dad

Emma and her neighborhood friends were bragging about their dads. "My father is really smart with computers," Thomas boasted. "One day last week, all the computers at his company shut down. Dad stayed overnight at work and got them back online."

Emma thought for a minute. She didn't want Thomas to think his dad was better than hers. "My dad is a fast runner," she said. "He runs in races. He has lots of ribbons from races when he has won first, second, or third place."

Brandon liked Thomas' father and Emma's father. But he knew his own dad was special, too. "My pop is a really good handyman," he said. "Everyone in the neighborhood knows he's the guy to call for help figuring out how to fix things."

As Thomas, Emma, and Brandon talked, they tried to "prove" to each other that their dads are important. But they forgot one important thing: their heavenly Father is greater than anyone else.

Your earthly dad is special, but your heavenly Father is best of any dad... and anybody!

Your Turn

1. Name some ways your earthly dad is special.
2. Why is your heavenly Father greater than anyone?

_____

_____

_____

_____

_____

_____

Prayer

Heavenly Father, You are the best! Amen.

#1 Dad

Color the ribbon to show that your heavenly Father is the #1 Dad!

God Is Our Father

God is the Father of us all.
O LORD, you are our Father ...
we are all the work of your hand.

~ Isaiah 64:8

Mrs. Hall's Sunday School Class

Mrs. Hall's Sunday school class was learning about how Jesus taught His disciples to pray.

"When Jesus prayed, He began by saying, 'Our Father,'" said Mrs. Hall.

Katie listened carefully. She had never met her own dad. Could she call God her Father, like Jesus did?

Katie raised her hand. "Does that mean Jesus shares His Father with us? I mean, why didn't Jesus pray 'My Father' instead of 'Our Father'?" she asked.

"Good question!" said Mrs. Hall. "We each have earthly families, don't we? And they're all different."

Katie looked around the table at her classmates. Charlie lived with his aunt. Jack had a stepmother. Andy was Lucy's cousin, but each of them had their own families, too. Mrs. Hall was right.

"Each of us is also a member of God's family," Mrs. Hall went on. "We share the same heavenly Father as Jesus."

Charlie looked surprised. "Does that mean that Jesus is actually our brother?" he asked.

Mrs. Hall smiled. "Yes. God is the Father of us all. That means Jesus is our brother. So when you pray the Lord's Prayer, you can say, 'Our Father' right along with Jesus."

Your Turn

1. Describe what you think about Jesus being your brother.
2. Why are you part of God's family?

_____

_____

Prayer

Our Father, I'm glad that I'm part of Your family, and that I have Jesus as my brother. Amen.

God's Family

Fill in the names of people you know who are in God's family!

God lives in heaven and in my heart.

This, then, is how you should pray:
Our Father **in heaven,**
hallowed be your name,

your kingdom come,
your will be done
on earth as it is in heaven.

Give us today our daily bread.

Forgive us our debts,
as we also have forgiven our debtors.

And lead us not into temptation,
but deliver us from the evil one.

~ *Matthew 6:9-13*

God is Alive!

Jesus is Alive!

**After He died, Jesus appeared to lots of people
and then went to heaven.**

*He was taken up before their very eyes,
and a cloud hid him from their sight.*

~ Acts 1:9

An Eyewitness Report

An "eyewitness" is a person who sees something happen. When you notice that the class bully sticks out his foot so that another student trips and falls, you become an eyewitness.

Your teacher may ask you to explain what you saw. What you tell her becomes an "eyewitness report."

Jesus' friends were eyewitnesses, too. They saw Jesus alive after He *died*. That is awesome. Some people have a hard time believing it's true, though. But God wanted us to know that Jesus is alive, so He had Jesus' friends write an eyewitness report.

In their report, Jesus' friends explain what they saw after Jesus died. They tell how Jesus came back to see them. He talked with them and he let them touch Him so they knew He was real. He even ate with them to show them He was a person. They saw Him rise to heaven.

Jesus wanted them to be eyewitnesses to the truth that He is alive! And He wants you to know all about it, too. You can read their report for yourself in John 20-21.

Your Turn

1. Why can it be hard for people to believe that Jesus is alive?
2. How does having an eyewitness report help you believe?

_____

_____

_____

_____

Prayer

God, thank You for giving me an eyewitness report that Jesus is alive!
I believe. Amen.

Your Eyewitness Report

Write or draw your own eyewitness report. Tell one thing you've seen God do!

Eyewitness Report

Jesus Sends the Holy Spirit

Jesus sends the Holy Spirit to live in me.

I will ask the Father, and he will give you another
Counselor to be with you forever–the Spirit of truth.

~ John 14:16-17

An Old Friend

Leah sat on the edge of her parents' bed while Mom packed a suitcase. Leah tried not to cry. Mom had to go on a work trip. She would be gone for a whole week. To Leah, a week felt like forever.

Mom saw Leah's sad face. "Leah, I have a special favor to ask you," said Mom. She held her favorite sweater out to Leah. "Would you please take care of my favorite sweater this week?" she asked.

The sweater wasn't fancy. In fact, it was old. Two buttons were missing and the elbows were frayed, but Mom wore it every evening as she prepared supper. She called it her "Old Friend."

"But don't you want to take it with you?" asked Leah.

Mom smiled. "I have to wear office clothes all the time on my trip. I won't need Old Friend. And I want to leave you something that helps you feel close to me."

Leah took the sweater from her mom. "Thank you, Mom!" she said. She rubbed the sweater to her cheek. "This helps a lot. Old Friend reminds me of you!"

Jesus had to go back to heaven to live with the Father. His disciples were sad. They would miss Jesus! But Jesus promised He wouldn't leave them alone. He sent the Holy Spirit to live with them. The Holy Spirit is like Jesus. He lives in your heart forever when you trust Jesus.

Your Turn

1. Why did Leah's mom give Leah the Old Friend?
2. Why did Jesus send the Holy Spirit to His disciples?
3. When does Jesus send the Holy Spirit to live in you?

Prayer

Lord Jesus, thank You for sending the Holy Spirit to live in me. Amen.

How Long Does the Holy Spirit Live?

Put an X through the first letter. Circle the second letter. Repeat the pattern for all the letters. When you're done, write the circled letters on the line to answer this question:

How long does the Holy Spirit live? *Puzzle solutions appear at the back of the book.*

E F G O K R B E C V H E U R J

_____ _____ _____ _____ _____ _____!

Jesus Lives in Me

Jesus is alive in me.

Christ lives in me. The life I live in the body, I live by faith in the Son of God, who loved me and gave himself for me.

~ Galatians 2:20

Tara Picks Her Fish

Tara rested her chin on her desk. She studied the fish swimming back and forth in the fish tank.

Just last week, she'd gone to the pet store with the allowance she'd saved for a month. She'd looked at all the different kinds of fish. Finally, she picked which ones she wanted and bought them with her own money.

Her fish were beautiful! Three angelfish swayed lazily back and forth in the tank. A school of guppies darted through the plants. Tara leaned closer, and the largest goldfish stared back at her. She sprinkled some fish food in the tank. The fish hurried to the top of the water for their meal.

Tara's fish were alive and growing in her fish tank. They trusted Tara to give them food and care for them so they could continue to be healthy and grow.

Tara paid for her fish with her own money. Jesus paid a price for you, too. When you tell Jesus you want to be His girl, He comes to live inside you. He wants you to have a strong, healthy faith. You can trust Him to help you keep growing closer to Him. Read your Bible, pray, and listen for Jesus' voice. It makes Jesus happy to be alive in you!

Your Turn

1. Why did Jesus have to pay a price for you?
2. Why does Jesus want to live inside you?
3. How can having Jesus in your heart help you grow?

_____

_____

_____

_____

Prayer

Lord Jesus, WOW! Thank You for paying the price for my sins so I can be close to You. Please be alive in my heart. Amen.

Jesus Living in Me

On each fish, write a way you can grow a strong faith when Jesus lives in you.

Jesus is Always with Me

I can be close to Jesus now and in heaven.
*I will come back and take you to be with me
that you also may be where I am.*

~ John 14:3

The Family Signal

Brooke's father got a job in a different city. He had to start work right away, but the family couldn't move into their new house for three more weeks.

Brooke's father had an idea. "I will move, start my job, and stay in a hotel until our house is ready," he said to the family. "You keep living here until our house is ready. Then, I'll come back and get you."

"I think we can make it work," said Brooke's mom. "We'll talk to Dad all the time."

"And we'll have a special family signal so you know when it's time to move," said Brooke's father. "You'll know we'll be together when I call up and say, 'It's time to load the boxes!'"

Brooke spoke on the phone with her father every day. A week went by. Then two weeks. But her father never gave the special signal.

Then one day, the telephone rang. Brooke answered. "It's time to load the boxes!" said Brooke's father. "I'm coming to get you. We're going to be together in our new house." That afternoon, his car pulled into the driveway. Brooke's father kept his promise.

Jesus is the same way. He keeps His promises. He wants to talk with you every day so He can be close to you. And you can be with Him forever.

Your Turn

1. How does it feel when you're apart from the people you love?
2. Have you ever thought about how great it will be to be with Jesus forever?
3. How can you know you'll be with Jesus forever?

_____

_____

Prayer

Lord, thank You for keeping Your promises. I want to be with You now and forever. Amen.

With You Forever

Someone wants to be with you forever. Find the name Jesus in the word search below. *Puzzle answers appear at the back of the book.*

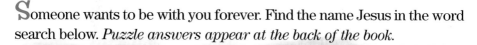

```
J B X T O K A I
D W G J F S B T
E Y R S M I R L
U J O S A J Q U
L E H P O E I P
V S L E N S G H
A Q U S Z U O C
A U S W I S P V
Z P E J K Y U B
F N J T X R A O
C O Y Q V W Z D
W B S U S E R I
```

Jesus is God's Right Hand Man

Jesus talks to God about my needs.

*Stephen ... looked up to heaven and saw the glory of God,
and Jesus standing at the right hand of God.*

~ Acts 7:55

A True Team

Maggie was excited. It was the first day of summer vacation. Her father had invited her to come to his new office so he could take her out to lunch.

Maggie knocked on her father's office door. She opened it slowly. A man sat next to her father at the desk. He was speaking to her dad. He sounded smart.

Her father looked up. "Maggie, come in!" he said. "I'd like you to meet Mr. West. He's my right hand man!"

Later, when Maggie and her father were seated at the restaurant, she asked him about Mr. West. "What did you mean when you said he's your right hand man?" she asked.

Her dad smiled. "Mr. West has been with the company a long time," he explained. "He tells me important information. I count on Mr. West. That's why I call him my right hand man. We're a true team."

Jesus is at God's side right now. The Bible says, "Christ Jesus... is at the right hand of God and is also interceding for us" (Romans 8:34). That means Jesus is talking to God for you about things that are important to you. He's asking God to help you.

God and Jesus are a team. God the Father listens to Jesus. Jesus is His right hand man!

Your Turn

1. Why can we be sure that Jesus is next to God right now?
   (Hint: look at the scripture verse)
2. How does it make you feel to know that Jesus talks to God about your needs?

_____

_____

Prayer

Lord Jesus, I worship You. You and God the Father are a team, and You care about me. I'm grateful. Amen.

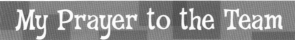

My Prayer to the Team

Write what's important to you. Then share your prayer with Jesus.

Dear Lord Jesus,
I've been thinking about

I'm not sure how to pray about it.
But I know that You understand.
Show me what to do.

Thank You.
Amen.

Jesus' Special Book

**When I believe in Jesus, He writes
my name down in the Book of Life.**

Rejoice that your names are written in heaven.

~ Luke 10:20

Jayme Goes to Camp

Jayme and Connor stood in line to check in to basketball camp. The gym was crowded, but at last, the twins were getting close to the front of the line.

"I heard that the camp is full," said the kid standing behind the twins. "The leaders can't allow anyone to attend who didn't sign up ahead of time."

Just then, the girl standing in front of Jayme reached the check-in table. "I don't understand," said the girl. "Why can't I attend camp?"

"Your name isn't on the list," said the coach. "Did you sign up ahead of time?" The girl shook her head sadly.

"I'm sorry," said the coach. "Only those whose names are on this list can attend." The girl walked away, disappointed.

Jayme and Connor weren't worried, though—they had planned ahead. They had signed up early to attend the basketball camp. When the time came for camp to begin, they were on the list.

There's a list of people who will live with Jesus forever. They've decided they want to be with Jesus and follow Him always. Jesus' list is called the Book of Life.

You can be on Jesus' list when you believe in Him and ask Him to be Lord of your life. Jesus will write your name in the Book of Life. You'll be with Jesus forever!

Make sure you're on the list: Talk to Jesus today.

Your Turn

1. Have you told Jesus you believe in Him?
2. Do you want Jesus to be Lord of your life?
3. Why is it important to talk with Jesus about what you believe?

_____

_____

_____

Prayer

Lord, I believe in You and I want to follow You. Amen.

The Book of Life

Write your name in the Book of Life. You can also write names of people you know who believe in Jesus, too!

Heaven is God's Home

**God's home is in heaven, and His people
can live there with Him forever.**

Our God is in heaven.

~ Psalm 115:3

The Payne Family Comes to Visit

Emily heard the door bell ring. "They're here!" she said. Emily, her parents, and her brother Tyler went to the entry hall.

Dad opened the door. "Welcome!" he said. He shook Mr. Payne's hand. Mom hugged Mrs. Payne. Emily counted the babies. One, two, three. The Paynes had triplets.

"Thank you for letting us stay," said Mr. Payne. "It's kind of you to invite us. You don't know us. Plus, we have three babies!"

"But we feel like we've known you a long time," said Emily. "We heard about you at church." The Paynes were missionaries. They lived in India and helped the people there learn about Jesus. Now, they were home for a break, but they needed a place to stay.

Everyone climbed the stairs to the guest rooms. "How pretty!" said Mrs. Payne. She saw the vase of flowers and a basket of snacks. "There are so many special touches that make this a home."

Mom put her hand on Mrs. Payne's shoulder. "We're glad you're here. We've got plenty of room, and we hope you'll think of our home as yours," she said.

Emily and her family liked having the Paynes stay in their home. God lives in heaven. Heaven is God's home. He shares it with all who choose to believe in Him.

Your Turn

1. Describe a time when you stayed at someone's home.
2. Why does God welcome His people to His home?

_____

_____

_____

_____

Prayer

Father, heaven is Your home. I'm glad You want to share it with Your people. Amen.

God's Home

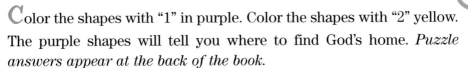

Color the shapes with "1" in purple. Color the shapes with "2" yellow. The purple shapes will tell you where to find God's home. *Puzzle answers appear at the back of the book.*

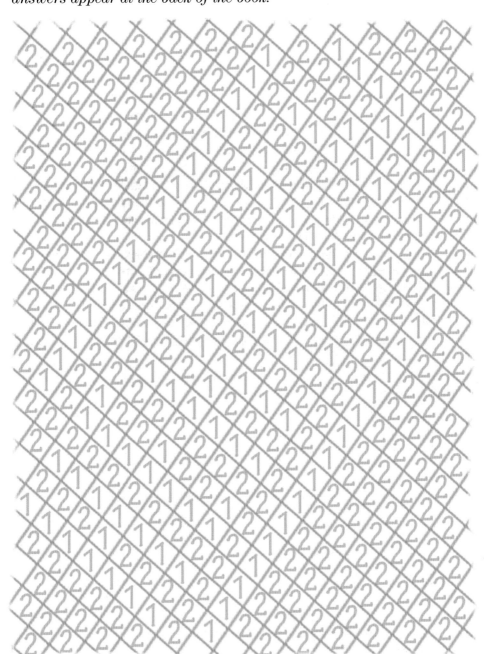

Heaven is a Real Place

Heaven is a real place and Jesus is there.
*(Jesus said), "You know the way
to the place where I am going."*

~ John 14:4

We'll All Be Changed

If heaven is a real place, why can't you go there to see it right now?

There are things you do to get ready when you go to a new place. You study a map. You look at photos. You talk with people who have been there. And most important, you ask for directions about how to get there.

Heaven is a real place. But going to heaven is different from going to the beach or taking a trip to the mountains. The Bible tells us that we get there a special way.

The Apostle Paul wrote, "I tell you a mystery...we will all be changed" (1 Corinthians 15:51). That means you can't travel to heaven in a car or on an airplane, like usual. Instead, when God is ready for you to go to heaven, He will change you and give you a new body for the trip.

Heaven isn't on one of your maps, because when you go you'll have a different set of eyes. That's why there aren't photos of heaven. When you go there, you'll look at things in a different way.

But there is one way you can get ready for your big trip to heaven. You can get directions from Jesus. Jesus said, "Whoever lives and believes in me will never die" (John 11:26). Believe in Jesus and live in Him. You'll be ready for your big trip!

Your Turn

1. Why do you want to know who God is?
2. How can you get ready for heaven?

Prayer

Lord Jesus, I believe in You. Help me walk with You and be close to You. I trust that when the time comes, You'll show me the special way to get to heaven. Amen.

Trip to Heaven

Tell Jesus you believe Him and want to live with Him. Draw a line to Jesus in heaven! *Puzzle answers appear at the back of the book.*

Heaven has Room for Me

Jesus makes sure there's room for me in heaven.

In my Father's house are many rooms; if it were not so, I would
have told you. I am going there to prepare a place for you.
~ John 14:2

Ellie Rides the Bus

Ellie climbed on the school bus and looked for a place to sit down. The Jones kids sat in the first row. Behind them, the Bates twins filled up a seat.

"Please sit down, Ellie, so we can keep moving," said the bus driver. But the bus was crowded! Ellie started to panic.

Then she saw a hand waving near the back of the bus. "Ellie, back here," a voice called. It was Morgan! Her friend had saved her a seat.

Morgan thought ahead. She was ready when Ellie got on the bus. Jesus does the same thing for you, too. You may think that there's not going to be a place for you in heaven, but when you're Jesus' friend, He's got things all worked out for you. He's getting a room ready for you in heaven right now!

Your Turn

1. What does it feel like when there's no room for you?
2. Why does Jesus want you to know He's getting a room ready for you in heaven?

_____

_____

_____

_____

Prayer

Lord, I'm thankful that You're thinking ahead and that You want me to have a place with You in heaven. I love You and I want to be with You forever. Amen.

My Room

Draw a picture of yourself in the room below, and think about the room Jesus is preparing for you.

God's Names tell what He's like.

This, then, is how you should pray:
Our Father in heaven,
hallowed be your name,

your kingdom come,
your will be done
on earth as it is in heaven.

Give us today our daily bread.

Forgive us our debts,
as we also have forgiven our debtors.

And lead us not into temptation,
but deliver us from the evil one.

~ Matthew 6:9-13

God's Names

God's Good Names

**God has different names, and each one explains
a different side of His character.**

*The name of the LORD is a strong tower;
the righteous run to it and are safe.*

~ Proverbs 18:10

A Name That Fits

Dan was named after his father, Danny, and his grandfather, Daniel.

Michaela's parents have a close friend, Michael, who helped them during a hard time in their lives. To honor him, they named their daughter "Michaela."

Noelle's parents hadn't picked a name for her. When she was born on Christmas Day, they chose "Noelle"—the French word for "Christmas."

Your parents chose your name. Maybe you were named for a family member or to honor a special person. Maybe your parents simply liked how your name sounded.

Things were different in Bible times. Babies weren't named right away when they were born. Instead, parents waited to see what a child was like. Then, parents gave the child a name that fit. Names matched a person's character.

That's one reason that there are so many names for God in the Bible. In Bible times, people understood that a name was really a piece of information about a person. Each of God's names tells you something about His character—what He is like. For instance, "Almighty God" means God is all powerful. "Savior" means God is the One who saves you from the mistakes you make. God has lots of wonderful traits.

The Bible says, "The name of the Lord is a strong tower" (Proverbs 18:10). In other words, "God's traits are strong and give you protection." You can study God's names to learn what He is like, and discover how God's names show He's Someone you can count on!

Your Turn

1. How were children named in Bible times?
2. What do God's names tell us?
3. Why can it be helpful to learn about God's names?

_____

_____

_____

Prayer

Lord God, You are so big and strong. There is so much I don't know about You, but I want to learn. Help me to understand Your names and know You better. Amen.

My Good Name

Fill in your name tag below!

My name

Why my parents chose my first name

My middle name

Why my parents chose my middle name

A good name is more desirable than great riches. (Proverbs 22:1)

God's Name is Honored

I honor God when I honor His name.
At the name of Jesus every knee should bow,
in heaven and on earth and under the earth.
~ Philippians 2:10

Penny Visits the Queen

Melissa's cousin Penny was visiting from England. Penny showed Melissa photos of her trip to Buckingham Palace, the home of the queen.

"I was invited to a special party," Penny explained. "I wore a new dress."

Melissa pointed to a picture of the queen talking with some children. "What happened?" she wanted to know. "What was it like to see the queen in person?"

"We knew when she walked into the room. Everyone bowed or curtsied. It looked like a wave of people going down on their knees!" Penny answered.

What Penny described for Melissa is one way people in England honor their queen: They bow.

Jesus taught us one way to honor God. He said that when we pray, we should say, "Our Father in heaven, hallowed be your name" (Matthew 6:9). To "hallow" God's name means to honor it and recognize it is holy. That means when you talk to God or about God, you only use respectful words.

When you honor God's name, it's as if you bow down on your knees to Him!

Your Turn

1. Why does bowing show respect?
2. What are some ways you can respect and honor God's name?
3. How is honoring God's name like bowing to Him?

_____

_____

_____

_____

Prayer

Lord, I'm bowing to You (bow your knees). Hallowed be Your name. Amen.

Every Knee Should Bow

The Bible says that "At the name of Jesus every knee should bow" (Philippians 2:10). Circle the people who need to hear about Jesus, so they will know to bow.

God is the Holy One

God can help me grow to be more holy.

"To whom will you compare me? Or who is my equal?"
says the Holy One.

~ Isaiah 40:25

Burnt Chicken

Shaniqua forgot to tell her mom that the stove bell rang. Now, the chicken in the oven was burned. Shaniqua felt badly, but was mad that her family blamed her for the mistake. "Nobody's perfect!" yelled Shaniqua.

Shaniqua was right and wrong.

None of us is perfect. But God is perfect!

That's what the Bible means when it says, "God is holy." Holy means "set apart" from the rest. In other words, God is different from people because He only does good things and never makes mistakes.

As you grow closer to God, He helps you make fewer mistakes. He wants you to become more holy. Ask Him to help you!

Shaniqua and her mom talked about how God could help her be more responsible and not lose her temper. They prayed together.

A few days later, Shaniqua was in the kitchen. She heard the stove bell ring. "OK, God," she prayed. "I want You to work in my heart. I want to be holy. Help me do the right thing." Shaniqua told her mom that dinner was ready. When her sisters teased her about letting the dinner burn the last time, she laughed it off. God worked in Shaniqua's heart. Shaniqua grew a little more holy that day!

Your Turn

1. What does "holy" mean?
2. Why does "being holy" seem like such a big job?
3. How can God help you become more holy?

_____

_____

_____

Prayer

Lord, You are the Holy One. You are set apart! Teach me how to call on You for help. I want to grow to be more holy. Amen.

How to Be Perfect?

It can be tempting to think you can become perfect by working at it on your own, but the fact is, you can't. Instead, try the way that works. Replace each number with the letters in the key. You'll see how you can get there the right way! *Puzzle solutions appear at the end of the book.*

I'm not perfect but the

____ ____ ____ ____   ____ ____ ____
1   6   3   2   6   8   4

can change me!

8 = N	1 = H
6 = O	3 = L
2 = Y	4 = E

God is Immanuel

Jesus is "God with us"— He's with me and shows me what God is like.

They will call him "Immanuel"— which means, "God with us."

~ Matthew 1:23

Brian Comes Home

The phone rang. Kayla picked it up. "Brian!" she shouted. "It's so good to hear your voice." Kayla's older brother, Brian, was in the military. He worked in another country.

Kayla wrote letters to Brian. Sometimes she talked with him on the phone. They also sent e-mails back and forth, but it just wasn't the same as being with him. Kayla hadn't seen Brian for four months.

"Is Mom home?" asked Brian. "And what about Dad?"

"Sure, I'll get them in a sec. You sound so clear, like you're just next door," said Kayla. "Where are you?"

Brian laughed. "I'm right here, sis," he said. Kayla turned.

Brian walked in the front door, holding his cell phone. "Surprise!" Kayla ran to hug her brother.

God is with us all the time, but God understands that it's hard for people to be apart from those they love. One big reason why He sent Jesus to earth was so we could see for ourselves what it's like to be with God. That's why one of God's names is "Immanuel" (ee-man-you-el). "Immanuel" means "God with us."

Your Turn

1. Why do people like being with those they love?
2. What's one reason God sent Jesus to live on earth?
3. How does having Jesus come to earth—your Immanuel, God with us—help you understand God better?

_____

_____

_____

_____

Prayer

God, thank You for being with me even when I don't know You're there. And thank You for sending Jesus—our Immanuel, God with us—so I can know You better. Amen.

Always with Us

Jesus came to earth and lived for a while. Now, He's back in heaven. Is He still our Immanuel (God with us)? Find out by substituting each number with the letter in the key. *Puzzle answers appear at the end of the book.*

Jesus said,

_____ _____ _____
  3   1   5

_____ _____ _____ _____ _____ _____
  1   4   10   1   11   7

_____ _____ _____ _____   _____ _____ _____.
 10   3   8   2   11   6   9

~ Matthew 28:20

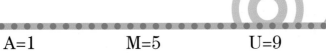

A=1	M=5	U=9
H=2	O=6	W=10
I=3	S=7	Y=11
L=4	T=8	

God is Spirit

I cannot see God the Spirit, but He can help me see Him at work.

God is spirit, and his worshipers must worship
in spirit and in truth.

~ John 4:24

You Can't See the Wind

"Look at the wind!" shouted Katie, standing at the front window. Trees swayed and leaves blew in circles. The flag hanging off Katie's front porch whipped around its pole twice. *Whoosh. Whee.* The wind whistled through the chimney.

Katie's older brother, Joshua, walked over to the window and stood next to her. "You can't see the wind," he protested. "It's invisible. Wind is air that's moving around."

Katie pointed to the shrubs in the yard. "But I can see our holly bushes moving back and forth," she said. "Isn't that the wind?"

Josh laughed. "You just answered your own question!" he said. "You said, 'I see the holly bushes moving.' You see what the wind *does* to the holly bushes—not the wind itself."

God's Spirit is like the wind. You may hear it, but you cannot see it. Katie and Joshua saw how the wind moved through their trees and bushes. You can do the same thing in order to see God's Spirit moving.

Look carefully. God's Spirit comes to people in ways you may not expect. Ask God to help you see His Spirit working in people. Ask God to help you worship Him and let His Spirit work in you. Then you can bend His way—just like the holly bushes in the wind.

Your Turn

1. Why did Katie think she could "see" the wind?
2. In what ways is God's Spirit like the wind?
3. How can you "see" God's Spirit at work?

_____

_____

_____

Prayer

Lord, I need Your help to see Your Spirit working. I need Your Spirit's help to worship You. I want You to work through me today. Amen.

Seeing the Spirit at Work

Fill in the blanks of the prayer, based on John 3:8.

Dear God,

I can hear the wind (pause and listen for a breeze or a blowing sound). I don't know where it comes from or how it forms.

But I know that the wind is real because I see it blowing through:

(look out your window and name things blowing in the wind).

I know Your Spirit is real because I see You working in

(name people who show the love of God to you).

I don't know what the wind will do next. And I don't know what Your Spirit will do next. But I am listening and watching. (Pause and listen quietly for how God wants to show Himself to you.)

Show me and help me see You at work today.

Amen.

God is My Rock

When I lean on God my Rock, I can stand firm.

He alone is my rock and my salvation;
he is my fortress, I will never be shaken.

~ Psalm 62:2

The Tree House

"I'm not sure you should try climbing up the tree house ladder right now," said Chad. "I still need to pour the concrete around the posts."

"Aw, come on," said Anna. "It looks good to me." Anna grabbed both sides of the ladder. She looked up at the tree house and took one step, then two. On the third step, Anna felt the ladder wobble. The tree house was shaking! She jumped down to the ground.

Chad pointed to the holes around the ladder's legs and the tree house posts. "The posts need to be secure to keep us safe," he said. "Come back on Wednesday, and try it again." Anna nodded.

Two days later, Anna stood in Chad's backyard. Chad showed her where he had poured concrete around the posts. Anna walked around the tree house. She put her arms around every post. She tried to shake the posts. They were secure! Even the ladder felt strong and steady. She and Chad climbed up the ladder.

Concrete helped make Chad's tree house secure. It was strong and couldn't be moved.

God is like that. The Bible says, "God is my rock." He can't be shaken.

Your Turn

1. Name a time when things around you changed and it was hard.
2. How can it help to have something secure to hang on to during hard times?
3. Why is God like a rock?

_____

_____

_____

Prayer

Lord, I'm glad you are strong and secure. You can't be shaken. You are my Rock! Amen.

My Rock

Create a special reminder that you can count on God.

What you need:

1. a small rock or stone
2. newspapers
3. smock (men's long-sleeved shirts work well)
4. acrylic paints
5. paint brush
6. markers

What to do:

Wash your rock or stone. Let it dry thoroughly. Spread newspapers on your work area. Use acrylic paints to paint your rock. Allow paint to dry completely. With markers, write "God is my Rock" on the painted rock.

Keep your rock in a special place to remind you that you can count on God—He is strong and will never be shaken!

God is My Light

God shows me the way to go and helps me make good choices.

(Jesus) said, "I am the light of the world. Whoever follows me will never walk in darkness, but will have the light of life."

~ John 8:12

The Camping Trip

Marissa woke up in her tent during the first night of camp. It was dark outside. She had to use the bathroom, but she knew she should take a buddy. "Chloe," she whispered to her friend, "are you awake?" Chloe groaned. "Yes," she said.

Marissa grabbed her flashlight. The girls crept outside and walked down the path. They heard talking and laughter to the right. "I forget which way we went earlier, but it sounds like there are people down there," said Chloe, pointing toward the noise. "The bathhouse must be that way." The girls turned to the right.

There were shadows along the path. Nothing looked familiar. Marissa shook her head. "This doesn't seem right," she said, flicking on the flashlight.

"We listened to the noise and took a wrong turn," said Chloe. "I'm glad you've got the flashlight. Let's go back and get it right this time."

Marissa and Chloe learned how easy it is to get lost. They followed other people's voices and assumed it was the right way, but when they finally turned on their light, they were able to get back on track.

God is your Light. He helps you make good choices. When you read the Bible, pray, and listen to the Holy Spirit, it's as if you're turning on a flashlight from God. He will help you stay on the right path when you take His Light with you along the way.

Just remember to turn on the Light before you make that wrong turn!

Your Turn

1. Marissa took her flashlight. Why did she get lost?
2. How does light help you see when it's dark?
3. How can God, your Light, help you each day?

_____

_____

_____

Prayer

Lord, You are my Light. Help me to remember to turn to You each day so You can guide my steps and keep me on the right path. Amen.

Don't Block the Light

What happens when light is blocked? How can you keep God's Light in your life? Follow the activity directions to find out.

What you need:

1. a dark room
2. a flashlight
3. assorted objects, like a piece of paper, a pencil and a spoon
4. a partner

What to do:

Ask your parents for permission to do this activity. You could invite one of them to join you as your partner!

Gather your materials. Go into the dark room, such as a bathroom with no windows, and shut the door.

Turn on the flashlight. Shine it onto a wall, door, or other surface.

Have your partner hold up one of the objects in front of the flashlight beam. What happens to the light on the wall?

Have your partner lower the object so that the flashlight beam is not blocked. What happens to the light in the room?

Repeat these steps using all the other objects.

God is Light. Name things that get in the way of His Light shining in your life. How can you keep His Light at full power?

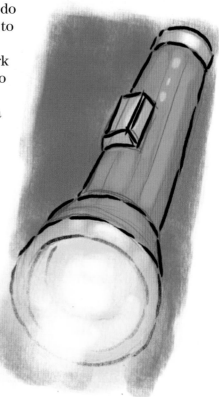

God is My Shepherd

God knows me, cares for me, watches over me and protects me.
The LORD is my shepherd, I shall not be in want.

~ Psalm 23:1

Nellie's Lost Puppy

Andrea's cocker spaniel, Nellie, had five puppies. "They are so cute!" cried Andrea. "Please, Dad, may I keep them?"

Dad laughed. "Yes," he said. "If you take care of them."

Every morning, Andrea walked out to the barn where Nellie and her pups slept. She took Nellie and the puppies to a field behind the barn. As it got dark, she gathered them up in a garden cart, since by then they were too tired to walk. One, two, three, four, five puppies, she counted every night.

One day, it began to rain. Andrea heard thunder and knew she had to get the puppies back to the barn right away! *One, two, three, four …* where was Shasta, the fifth puppy?

Andrea hurried through the grass. "Shasta!" she called. She stopped to listen. Was that a whimper? Andrea ran to the fence at the back of the field. There was a spot where the fence slats had broken. Shasta was stuck beneath the boards and couldn't get out. The puppy was shaking.

"Silly Shasta!" cried Andrea, relieved. She pulled the puppy to safety.

In Bible times, shepherds cared for sheep in the same way. Each sheep was valuable to the owner. A shepherd's job was to know each sheep by name, watch over the flock and keep them safe. That's why one of God's names is "Shepherd." He knows you, cares for you and watches over you.

Your Turn

1. Name the ways Andrea cared for Nellie and her pups.
2. How was Andrea like a shepherd?
3. Why does God call Himself your "Shepherd"?

Prayer

Lord, You are my Shepherd. Thank You for knowing me, caring for me, watching over me, and protecting me. Amen.

Find the Lost Sheep

God knows His sheep. He will find them. Circle the five lost sheep in the picture. *Puzzle solutions appear at the back of the book.*

God is My Teacher

God teaches me how to live.
*(Jesus said), "You call me 'Teacher' and 'Lord,'
and rightly so, for that is what I am."*

~ John 13:13

What Do You Want to Do When You Grow Up?

"What do you think you might like to do when you grow up?" asked Mrs. Davis, Grace's school teacher. "Write down a list of ideas."

Students in the class began to write, but Grace raised her hand. "I don't know what I want to do when I get older," she said.

Mrs. Davis smiled. "Start by listing things you like to do now," she said. Grace wrote,

I like school—Mrs. Davis makes me want to learn because she cares.

I like piano lessons—Ms. Johnson, my teacher, always gets me excited about music.

I like softball—Coach Gibson helped our team win the tournament, even though we weren't good at the beginning of the season.

I like Sunday school—Mrs. White does fun crafts and games with us.

Mrs. Davis looked over Grace's shoulder. "I see a big clue that you've given yourself, Grace," she said. "You have lots of different kinds of teachers. You like the different ways they help you learn."

"Hmmm," said Grace. "Maybe I should think about being a teacher." She studied her list. Each teacher had a special way of helping her to learn and become more confident in her abilities.

The Bible tells us that God is our Teacher.

Grace's teachers taught her in different ways. God uses different ways to help you learn about Him. He is your Teacher.

Your Turn

1. Name your teachers. What makes each one special or different?
2. What are some different ways God helps you learn?

_____

_____

Prayer

God, thank You for helping me to learn by (name different ways He helps you learn). You are my Teacher! Amen.

Help Me Learn

Look at each picture, and describe how each situation is an opportunity to learn.

God is My Savior

God saves me when I call on His name.
Praise be to the Lord, to God our Savior,
who daily bears our burdens.

~ Psalm 68:19

The Rescue Demonstration

At the boatyard, Emma and her family watched a rescue demonstration. A swimmer fell in the water. He waved his hands. "Help!" he shouted.

Emma saw another sailor jump out of the boat to rescue his friend. A worker on the boat threw the rescuer a life preserver, which he gave to their fallen friend. Both men swam back to the boat safely.

"He saved his friend's life!" said Emma.

A savior rescues another person from danger. Emma saw how the sailor saved his friend from drowning in the water.

Every day, you can choose to live the right way or the wrong way. God is your Savior. He can keep you from the danger of making bad choices. He can help you not say hurtful words. He can help you obey your parents rather than disobey them. He can help you to do your chores with a joyful heart, rather than forget, whine and complain.

Emma saw the swimmer wave his hands. He called out for help and his friend rescued him. You can call out to God your Savior every day. He will "jump in," rescue you and help you live the right way.

Your Turn

1. What did the swimmer do to get help?
2. How can "making a mistake" in your daily life be dangerous?
3. What is one reason God is your "Savior"?

Prayer

Lord God, I know I need Your help to live the right way. I want to make good choices, say kind words, obey my parents, and be responsible for my chores. Help! I need You, O Savior. Amen.

God is My Life Preserver

Fill in each life preserver with an example of help you need today. Then pray each prayer to God your Savior!

God is King of kings in heaven, on earth, and in my heart.

This, then, is how you should pray:
Our Father in heaven,
hallowed be your name,

your kingdom come,
your will be done
on earth as it is in heaven.

Give us today our daily bread.

Forgive us our debts,
as we also have forgiven our debtors.

And lead us not into temptation,
but deliver us from the evil one.

~ Matthew 6:9-13

God is My King

My God is Super King

God is King over everyone and everything.

God reigns over the nations; God is seated on his holy throne.

~ Psalm 47:8

King of Kings

"Once upon a time, a king ruled over the land." This is how a lot of fairy tales begin. What do you think of when you hear the word king? You may be think of a king as a person in a fairy tale. The king sits on a throne and wears a crown. He rides a white horse and rules over his people. A good king does good things for his people.

In the United States, we don't have a king who rules over us. We have a president and a congress, that we elect. But some nations still have a king as their leader. In these countries, the king rules the country and makes all of the decisions.

Mix all those jobs of a king together and you'll have a good idea of what it means that God is King! God sits on His throne in heaven. God leads His people, and because He is always good, we can trust Him to make good decisions for us.

But there's one more important thing that God our King does that other kings do not do. God is the Head of *all* the kings. He's in charge of *all* the nations. The Bible says, "God (is) the blessed and only Ruler, the King of kings and Lord of lords" (1 Timothy 6:15).

God is the Super King!

Your Turn

1. When you think of a "king," what ideas come to your mind first?
2. What makes God the Super King of all kings?

_____

_____

_____

_____

_____

Prayer

God, You are Ruler and Leader of all. You are King of kings and I praise You! Amen.

God's Throne

Revelation 4:3 says that a rainbow encircles God's throne in heaven. Color God's rainbow!

My King Needs an Invitation

**I can invite God to rule
in my heart, my life, and my world.**
Come, Lord Jesus.
~ Revelation 22:20

Olivia's Birthday Party

"Olivia is having a birthday party on Saturday," said Kristen. "May I go?"

Mom thought a minute. "I didn't know that you are friends with Olivia," she said. "Did you get an invitation?"

Kristen hung her head. "No," she said sadly.

"You can go only if you're invited," said Mom.

God wants to be a part of your life. He wants to come to your "party," but He's not a "party crasher." He will only come if you want Him there. He will only come if He's invited.

When you pray to God, "Your kingdom come," you're sending God an invitation. You're saying to God, "I know that living with You is wonderful. I want You at my party. Please come and set up Your Kingdom here on earth. I want Your Kingdom to rule in my world."

Plus, you can invite God again and again. Each time you pray, "Your kingdom come," you're telling God you want more of Him in your heart, your life, and your world.

God won't force Himself on you. God needs an invitation from you to be in your life. Send Him one today!

Your Turn

1. Why does God need an invitation from you?
2. What happens when you send God an invitation?

_____

_____

_____

Prayer

Lord, I want more of You in my life. I invite You now. May Your kingdom come into my heart, my life and my world. Amen.

An Invitation to My King

Fill in the party invitation!

To:_____ **God my King**_____

From:_____
(Your name)

What:_____ **My Celebration**_____

When:_____
(Today's Date)

Where:**In my heart, my life, my world**

Why:_____
(Why you want God to attend)

My King Comes First

God wants me to put Him first so He can work through me.

Seek first his kingdom and his righteousness,
and all these things will be given to you as well.

~ Matthew 6:33

What to Wear?

Hillary studied the clothes hanging in her closet. She couldn't decide what to wear to school.

What about her jeans with the sequin pockets? They didn't match her new pink top. She could choose her black pants instead…but it was going to be warm today. Maybe she should wear shorts, or even a skirt? Oh, why was it so hard to choose? Hillary wrung her hands. This day wasn't starting well at all.

To Hillary, choosing her clothes was important. Maybe too important.

Jesus said, "Why do you worry about clothes? Your heavenly Father knows that you need them" (Matthew 6:28, 32).

God doesn't want Hillary to think more about what she wears than about Him. It's not because God is selfish. Instead, God knows that when He comes first for Hillary, then she'll be happier.

That's what Jesus meant when He said, "Seek first God's kingdom." He promises to make sure you have what you need. When you put God first, He's able to work through you in big ways.

Your Turn

1. What can stand in your way of putting God first?
2. Why is it important to put God first?

_____

_____

_____

_____

_____

Prayer

Lord, I confess that I've put (name something that's been more important to you than God) ahead of You. I'm sorry. Please forgive me. Help me to seek You first so Your Kingdom can grow. Amen.

God is First

Make a poster by tracing the words on a piece of paper. Color your poster. Put it in a special place to remind you to always keep God first in your life.

My King is Good

God rules His Kingdom with goodness.
*The people thought that the kingdom of God
was going to appear at once.*

~ Luke 19:11

King of the Castle

Bang. Smash. POW! "I'm king of the castle!" shouted Dave. He stood at the top of the dirt pile and waved his "sword," made from a stick. "I claim this hill. I will rule over it!" he announced triumphantly.

Madison laughed. Her brother had won the game. He had made it to the top of the dirt pile before her. "OK, King Dave," she said. "You win."

Dave and Madison's game, "King of the Castle," can help you understand God's kingdom. Like Dave and Madison, people in Jesus' time thought of a king as a person who rules over a land. The king had to fight to win the land. After that, the people had to obey the king.

But it was confusing to people when Jesus talked about the "Kingdom of God." The people couldn't see God riding a horse. They couldn't see God fighting with weapons.

We can't see "good" and "evil" in the same way we can see swords and weapons. But good and evil are real. God fights against evil so that good can rule in our hearts. He has already won the battle between good and evil, even though we can't see it!

God wants to be our leader and wants us to obey Him. God's Kingdom is special. You can choose to follow Him and have Him be your King!

Your Turn

1. Why can it be confusing to understand the Kingdom of God?
2. What battle has God our King already won?
3. Why does God let you choose to follow Him rather than forcing you?

Prayer

God, You have won the battle over evil. You are good. I want to follow You. I want You to be my King. Amen.

King of My Heart

Fill in your name to show that God is King of your heart!

God has won the fight
of good over evil.

God is King in

_____'s

heart!

My King is Awesome

God thought up ideas for everything that He put in His world.
How awesome is the LORD Most High,
the great King over all the earth!

~ Psalm 47:2

Brittany Visits the Mountains

Brittany was in the car. She and her family were on vacation. They drove a long time and eventually Brittany fell asleep.

"WOW!" When Brittany woke up, she saw that the view had changed. "WOW!" she exclaimed again. She saw large, purple mountains with pure white, snowy tops. "The mountains are awesome!" she said.

"Yes," said Dad. "And we're not even that close. You'll see how huge the mountains really are when we get nearer."

Brittany felt a tickle. She looked down. A tiny ant crept down her arm. "It looks like we picked up a visitor when we stopped for our picnic," she said, studying the ant. "It's so little," she said. "And the mountains are so big."

"Now, that's awesome," said her mom. "God made both of them!"

God is the Creator King. He thought up ideas of things that would be good to have on the earth: different kinds of land and mountains and rivers, different plants and animals, different colors and weather.

Then, after thinking up those ideas, God made all of them. He did it all by Himself. He is awesome!

Your Turn

1. What would it take for God to think up ideas for what to put in His world?
2. What would it take for God to make the things He put in His world?
3. Why is that awesome?

_____

_____

_____

_____

Prayer

Lord, You are awesome because (name some reasons you think He is awesome). I praise You! Amen.

God's Awesome World

With colored pencils, crayons or markers, draw pictures of things God made that are in His awesome world.

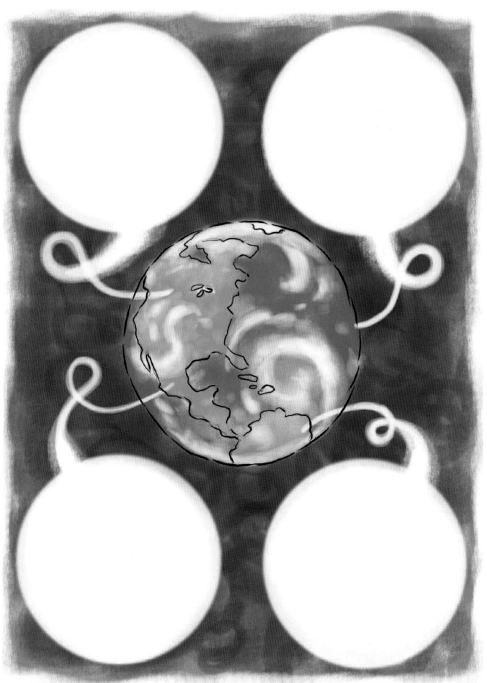

My King Lives in Me

When I tell God I need Him, God's Kingdom can live in me.

I live in a high and holy place,
but also with him who is contrite and lowly in spirit.

~ Isaiah 57:15

Amanda Makes Room for God

Amanda sat in church. She looked at the cross at the front. It was huge. She looked around her. There were many people. Amanda felt small—did she really matter to God?

Dear God, Amanda prayed. *I know You are great. But I'm just a girl. I have that problem with my stepfather… I can't handle it alone. I know that You are greater than that problem. Please help me.*

God lives in heaven, but God also wants to live in your heart.

He can come into your heart when you make room for Him. Amanda made room for God. She knew her problems were too big for her to handle alone, so she told God she needed Him. Amanda was humble before God.

You matter to God because He wants to live in you, love you and help you. When you humble yourself before God, He can live in you. You'll be a part of His Kingdom on earth!

Your Turn

1. How can you make room in your heart for God?
2. Why does God promise to answer a prayer like Amanda's?
   (Hint: look at the Bible verse)

_____

_____

_____

_____

_____

_____

Prayer

Lord God, You are King in heaven. I humble myself before You. I know You are great and that I need You. Make Your home in my heart. Amen.

God is Greater Than...

> is a special symbol. It means "greater than," or "bigger than." For example, 2 > 1 means "two is greater than one."

Use the "greater than" symbol to show how great God is! In the blanks below, write three things that God is greater than!

God > than

_____

_____.

God > than

_____

_____.

God > than

_____

_____.

My King Enjoys Me

God enjoys me and thinks I'm very special.
The LORD takes delight in his people;
he crowns the humble with salvation.

~ Psalm 149:4

Alexa and Corrie

"I like being with Corrie," Alexa told her mom. "But not Bethany."

If you're like Alexa, there are some people you enjoy. Corrie makes Alexa laugh. Alexa and Corrie have fun together. They talk easily and Alexa likes Corrie's sense of humor. They may not always agree about everything, but both girls listen to each other anyway.

On the other hand, Alexa feels uncomfortable around Bethany. For some reason, she and Bethany just don't connect. Alexa could hang around with Bethany, but if she did, she'd feel like she's just putting up with her. Alexa chooses not to spend time with Bethany.

Think about this: God likes you! He wants to be around you all the time. He wants to talk with you and listen to you. He's not just putting up with you—He likes you exactly the way you are. In fact, the Bible says that God enjoys you so much that He wants everyone to know that you're His friend.

The King of heaven takes delight in you! How awesome is that?

Your Turn

1. Do you ever feel like some people are just putting up with you?

2. Have you ever thought that God enjoys being around you? Why or why not?

3. In the Kingdom of God, people enjoy God and each other all the time. How is that different from the way things are for you now?

Prayer

Lord God, it feels so good to know that You enjoy me! I enjoy You, too. Amen.

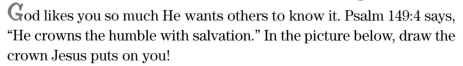

A Crown from My King

God likes you so much He wants others to know it. Psalm 149:4 says, "He crowns the humble with salvation." In the picture below, draw the crown Jesus puts on you!

My King Loves Through Me

When I love and care for others, I live out the Kingdom of God.

By this all men will know that you are my disciples,
if you love one another.

~ John 13:35

Kingdom Kids

Kelsie went to Kingdom Kids every Monday after school. Once she did all her homework, she got to play on the computer.

But today, Ryan sat at the computer. Kelsie walked over to the computer station and she stood next to Ryan. "When will you be done?" she asked.

Ryan didn't answer. He was thinking hard.

Kelsie felt irritated. "RYAN!" she said, louder this time. "When will you be done at the computer?"

"I dunno," said Ryan. He squinted his eyes at the screen. Then, he wrote some numbers on a piece of paper.

Why was Ryan being so annoying? Kelsie was losing her patience. Then, she remembered the story Mrs. Gates had told them today, during Kingdom Kids devotions, "Try to remember this story when you feel like you're losing your temper," said Mrs. Gates. She explained that Jesus' friends competed with each other, but He wanted His friends to care for one another. "You can show that God's Kingdom is alive in you when you're kind to each other," said Mrs. Gates.

Maybe I can help Ryan, Kelsie thought. Kelsie looked over Ryan's shoulder. She saw he was working on *Secret Mountain Math Adventure*. He was stuck in the second cave and he needed to solve a hard word problem.

Kelsie had an idea. She moved a chair next to Ryan. "Would you like some help?" she asked.

Ryan looked at her, surprised. "Yeah, sure," he said gratefully.

Your Turn

1. Why was Kelsie annoyed at first?
2. What made Kelsie act differently?
3. Why does being kind to other people show that God's Kingdom lives in you?

_____

_____

_____

Prayer

God, I want Your Kingdom to be alive in me. Help me show kindness to others today. Amen.

Ways to Show Jesus' Love

Look at the pictures and describe a way someone in each situation below has an opportunity to show Jesus' love!

My King Makes Me Happy

I'm part of God's winning team here on earth, and that makes me happy.

Sing praises to our King, sing praises.
For God is the King of all the earth.

~ Psalm 47:6-7

Ebony's Team

Ebony jumped up and down as Latoya raced to home plate. Latoya was going to get another run for their softball team. They were going to win again!

Ebony's team had played ten games and won all of them. Now, they were going to compete against other teams in the state. "You have worked very hard," said Coach Jackson. "You have helped each other. You have had a positive attitude. You have listened to me when I gave you advice. You have each done your part. Because of that we have a winning team!"

It's fun to be on a winning team. It makes you happy. That's one reason it's so much fun to know God and be close to Him.

God is King over all the earth. You can follow His lead. You can do your part by obeying God and helping others—your team members. You can rejoice knowing He's the head of your winning team!

Your Turn

1. Why is it fun to be on a winning team?
2. What can you do to be a part of God's winning team on earth?

_____

_____

_____

_____

Prayer

God, I'm so happy I can be on Your team. Show me how to do my part for Your work here on earth. Amen.

Praise to the Head of the Team

Read the verses from Psalm 149. Circle the words that show different ways you can praise God your King, the head of your team! Hint: look for the action words.

Let Israel rejoice in their Maker;

let the people of Zion be glad in their King.

Let them praise his name with dancing

and make music to him with tambourine and harp.

(Psalm 149:2-3)

My King Answers Prayer

My heartfelt prayers are powerful.

The prayer of a righteous man is powerful and effective.

~ James 5:16

Melanie's Prayer

"Please God," Melanie pleaded. "Help Mr. Palmer not be angry or feel alone because Mrs. Palmer is sick." Melanie squeezed shut her eyes. A few tears trickled down her cheeks. She loved her neighbors, the Palmers. She knew Mr. Palmer was hurting inside ever since Mrs. Palmer had been diagnosed with cancer. She felt pain for both of them.

Melanie had strong feelings and she shared them with God. That made her prayer powerful. Melanie's prayer is the kind of prayer that allows God's work to grow here on earth.

What happens when you want to pray a powerful prayer, like Melanie's, but you don't have strong feelings? Be honest with God. Tell Him you want to pray a powerful prayer. Ask Him to help you pray from your heart deeply so that His Kingdom can grow. That kind of prayer has a special strength of its own, because it's truthful!

Your Turn

1. Have you ever prayed your strong feelings to God?
2. Why do you think God appreciates our prayers with strong feelings?
3. What makes truthful prayers so powerful?

_____

_____

_____

_____

_____

Prayer

Dear Lord, I want my prayers to have power for Your Kingdom. Help me pray truthfully and from my heart. Amen.

Prayers from My Heart

Write the name of a person who needs prayer in each section of the heart. Then pray a strong prayer for each one!

My King Is Coming

I can tell others that God wants to live in them.

Prepare the way for the Lord,
make straight paths for him.

~ Matthew 3:3

The New Baby

Claire was going to be a big sister! "The baby is coming any day now," said her mom. "We need to get ready."

Claire helped Mom. She folded clothes. She sorted toys. She helped Mom and Dad tell the neighbors that the baby was coming soon. Claire did an important job in helping get ready for her new brother!

John the Baptist knew that Jesus was coming. He knew that when Jesus came, it would be like having God's Kingdom living with them. He told the people, "The kingdom of heaven is near" (Matthew 3:2).

Some people made fun of John. Some didn't believe him and some ignored him. But some listened, and they were ready when Jesus came. They got to be part of the Kingdom of God!

You can be like Claire and like John the Baptist. You can tell others about Jesus by explaining that God's Kingdom is near. When you tell others that God wants to live in them, you can help grow God's Kingdom on earth!

Your Turn

1. How did John the Baptist help God's Kingdom?
2. Does everybody listen when they hear about God's Kingdom? Why or why not?
3. How can you help grow God's Kingdom on earth?

_____

_____

_____

_____

_____

Prayer

Lord, I pray that Your Kingdom will grow. Show me who to talk to about You. Amen.

Straight Paths to God's Kingdom

Help your friends find God's Kingdom. Draw the most direct, straight route! *Puzzle solutions appear at the back of the book.*

God's ways are best and
He helps me live them out.

This, then, is how you should pray:
Our Father in heaven,
hallowed be your name,

your kingdom come,
**your will be done
on earth as it is in heaven.**

Give us today our daily bread.

Forgive us our debts,
as we also have forgiven our debtors.

And lead us not into temptation,
but deliver us from the evil one.

~ Matthew 6:9-13

God's Ways

God Tells Me His Ways

**God wants me to follow His ways,
so He tells me about them in the Bible.**

*He made known to us the mystery of his will
according to his good pleasure.*

~ Ephesians 1:9

God's Way

Imagine you're at a friend's house. Your friend asks you to go to the kitchen and get her a glass of orange juice. "Please put some ice in it, too," she says.

Once you get to the kitchen, you don't know where to find the drinking glasses. The refrigerator is so full that you can't see the carton of juice, and your friend's ice maker is different from yours at home.

You want to do what your friend asked, but you don't know how. So what would you do in this situation? If you are anything like me, you'd probably start by opening up the cupboards and looking for a glass.

It's often like that with God: you may want to do things God's way, but you may be unsure of how to go about it.

God doesn't want you to be confused about Him. God's ways of doing things are special. But lots of times, His ways are different from ours. You might even think that His ways are mysterious and hard to figure out.

That's why He God gave us the Bible. The Bible explains God's ways, which are better than any other way.

Your Turn

1. Why can understanding God's ways be confusing?
2. Are you confused right now about one of God's ways? If so, write it down.
3. How can you find out God's ways?

_____

_____

_____

Prayer

God, I know Your ways are good. But right now, I don't understand (name one of God's ways that is confusing to you). Show me in the Bible what I need to understand this. Amen.

Plans Puzzle

Circle the words you find that describe "God's ways." *Puzzle answers appear at the end of the book.*

Z X Z X X Z Z X

P U R P O S E S

X W I L L Z X Z

Z X Z A Z X Z X

X Z X N X Z X Z

W A Y S Z X Z X

God's Ways Always Work

**God's ways worked in Jesus' time,
they work today, and they'll keep working.**
The plans of the LORD stand firm forever.
~ Psalm 33:11

Lauren's Good Decision

Lauren followed Shelby and Sam around to the back of their house. It was hot. She was glad her friends had invited her over to cool off in the backyard.

Lauren set down her towel away from the water sprinkler. "Where's the spigot?" she asked. "I'll turn on the water."

Suddenly Shelby had a funny look on her face. She turned away. Lauren saw Sam fumbling in his pocket. Something seemed different from before.

"What's going on?" asked Lauren.

Sam pulled out a small packet. "C'mon," he said. "Let's hide under the porch. We can try these. I snatched them from my dad. Our aunt is inside, but she's not paying attention. No one will know." Sam held up the pack of cigarettes.

Lauren gasped. She turned to Shelby. "I thought we were going to play water games," she said.

Shelby shrugged. "Our plans changed. Are you in or out?"

Lauren picked up her towel. "No, thanks," she said. "I'd rather stick to doing things the way I know they work."

"What do you mean?" asked Shelby.

"Like doing the right thing," said Lauren. "That always works."

Your Turn

1. Why does doing the right thing always work?
2. You have choices every day. When you're in a situation like Lauren's, how can you know to do things God's way?

_____

_____

_____

Prayer

God, teach me Your ways. Help me be ready to make good choices. I know Your ways always work. Amen.

The Way That Works

Jesus' ways always work. Find your way through the maze to Jesus!
Puzzle answers appear at the end of the book.

God Helps Me

God's ways may be hard for me to follow, but He helps me.

I can do everything through him who gives me strength.

~ Philippians 4:13

Aunt Doris

Mackenzie didn't want to go visit her great-aunt Doris.

Mackenzie's mother parked the car outside the apartment. Mackenzie groaned. "Why do I have to go in?" she asked.

"It's the right thing to do," said her mom.

Together, they climbed the stairs to the second floor. Aunt Doris' door was open. "Welcome!" she said, hugging Mackenzie and her mom. Suddenly, Mackenzie saw a ball of fur at Aunt Doris' feet.

Her great-aunt scooped up the wiggling kitten. "Do you like Felix?" she asked Mackenzie, handing the pet to her. "He's just two months old."

Mackenzie ran a finger down over Felix's fur. The kitten reached and batted her finger away. Mackenzie laughed.

"I got him to keep me company," said Aunt Doris. "But I thought you'd enjoy playing with him, too." She winked at Mackenzie.

Mackenzie looked up in surprise. Maybe Aunt Doris understood her better than she'd thought.

It was hard for Mackenzie to do the right thing and visit her great-aunt, but she did anyway. Aunt Doris was glad. She liked being with Mackenzie.

God's ways are right. He understands that it can be hard for you to go along with His ways. Another word for God's "ways" is God's "will." He'll help you do His will and follow His ways because He wants the best for you.

Your Turn

1. Name a time when you didn't feel like doing something but did it anyway, just because it was right to do it.
2. Why does God want you to do right things?
3. How will God help you do right things?

Prayer

Lord God, Your ways are good. Sometimes I don't want to do them, like (name a time when you didn't want to do the right thing). But help me to do Your will anyway. Amen.

The Right Way

Here's one way God helps you to do the right thing. Substitute each symbol for the letter in the key to solve the puzzle. *Puzzle answers appear at the end of the book.*

```
___   ___   ___   ___   ___
 +     $     !     @     %

___   ___         ___   ___
 *     $           +     (

___   ___
 #     (

___   ___   ___   ___
 ?     (     <     )

___   ___   ___   ___ .
 >     ^     &     &
```

~ Psalm 143:10

A = !
C = @
D = #
E = $
H = %
I = ^
L = &
M = *
O = (
R =)
T = +
U = <
W = >
Y = ?

God Wants Me to Be Thankful

I can thank God for everything—good things and bad things.

*Give thanks in all circumstances, for this is God's will
for you in Christ Jesus.*

~ 1 Thessalonians 5:18

Some Things are Hard

God wants you to be thankful, but He doesn't just want you to thank Him for your food, your home and for the people who love you. The Bible says, "Give thanks in all circumstances" (1 Thessalonians 5:18). "Circumstances" are the things happening around you.

It's easy to understand why God wants you to be thankful for good things that happen, like getting to go to a fun birthday party or learning how to make bead necklaces at school. But what about when things are hard?

Does God want you to be thankful when you get a D- on a science test? Does God want you to be thankful that your swim meet was canceled because of rain? Does God want you to be thankful that your bossy older brother yelled at you to pick up your library books?

God doesn't want you to fail your test or miss a game or be bossed around. The reason He wants you to be thankful in all things—both good things and bad things—is this: He wants to use every circumstance in your life to help you grow closer to Him and learn to do things His way.

Your Turn

1. Is it easier to thank God when things are good or when things are bad? Why?
2. Why does God want you to thank Him when things are hard?

_____

_____

_____

_____

Prayer

Lord God, show me how to grow from everything You put in my life. I'm thankful that You care about me and want me to do things Your way. Amen.

My Thankful List

*M*ake a list of hard things that happened to you today. Think of a way you can be thankful for each one. Give God thanks and ask Him to help you grow!

God Wants Me to Do Good

My good actions show God's love.

It is God's will that by doing good you should silence
the ignorant talk of foolish men.

~ 1 Peter 2:15

The Copycat

Lily's brother, John, was two years old. John liked to do the same things Lily did. It bothered Lily.

"He's a copycat," she complained, throwing down her book. John picked up the book. He threw it down. He smiled.

"That's how he learns," explained Mom. "He watches what you do. Then he does the same thing."

Lily thought for a minute. "Are you sure he's not doing it to make me mad?" she asked.

"I'm sure," said her mom. "But why don't you see for yourself? Do something kind, and see if he does it, too."

"OK," said Lily. She walked over to her mom. She hugged her mom. "I love you, Mom."

John watched. He toddled over to Mom. He grabbed Mom's legs. "Wuv you," he said.

Lily and Mom laughed. Mom hugged Lily and hugged John. "I wuv you, too," she said.

People are always watching how you treat others. When you are a Christian, you can show God's love by how you act toward people. That's one of the ways God works to spread His love. People will see God working through you. They will want to copy you!

Your Turn

1. Why was Lily mad?
2. What did Lily learn?
3. Can people see God's love in your actions? Why or why not?

Prayer

God, You want me to do good. Help me remember to show Your love in how I behave today. Amen.

Reflecting God's Love

Jesus was kind to the children. Draw a picture on the mirror of how you can reflect Jesus' love to other boys and girls.

God Wants Me to Help

God gives me special ways I can help others.

We are God's workmanship,
created in Christ Jesus to do good works.

~ Ephesians 2:10

Laurie Helps

Laurie stood on the front porch with her two brothers. Peter, the oldest, searched through his backpack for the house key. Mom had to work late, but Peter was old enough to watch Laurie and Nathan until she got home.

"Mom gave me the key this morning," Peter said. "But I can't find it."

Laurie shivered. It was getting colder.

Smash! Laurie turned back to Peter. He had dumped out everything from his backpack. "It's not here," he said, searching through papers.

"What will we do?" asked Nathan, pointing to the gray clouds. "We can't stay outside. I think a storm is coming."

Laurie thought quietly. Maybe she could help. "There's an extra key in the shed," she said.

"Duh, Laurie," said Peter. "But the shed's got a lock."

Laurie smiled. "I know the combination," she said, turning and walking towards the backyard. "Dad showed me. He said I'd remember it because I'm good with numbers."

She returned a few minutes later, holding up the key. "Thanks, kid," said Peter.

Laurie smiled. "Glad I could help," she said.

Your Turn

1. Why was Laurie able to help?
2. Have you ever thought that God created you for special times when you could help?
3. How can you be ready to help when you're needed?

_____

_____

_____

Prayer

Lord, I want to help in the special ways You plan for me. Help me to listen to You. Amen.

A Special Way I Can Help

How does God want you to help? Draw a picture below of a way you can help someone.

God Makes Me New

God wants to give me a new start each day.
If anyone is in Christ, he is a new creation;
the old has gone, the new has come!
~ 2 Corinthians 5:17

Holly's Fresh Start

Holly's mom stood in the bedroom doorway. Holly covered her face. She was ashamed. Today, Mom had caught her stealing two dollars from her purse.

Mom came in the room. She sat down next to Holly and hugged her.

"I'm so sorry, Mom," said Holly.

Mom smiled. "You've said that at least twenty times," she answered.

"I feel awful," said Holly. "I don't think you'll ever love me again."

Mom stood up. She walked over to Holly's calendar. She pointed to the date. "Give me a pen, Holly," she said. She took the black marker Holly handed her. She made an X through that day's box.

"You made a mistake today, Holly, but you were sorry for it," said Mom. Holly nodded. Mom pointed to the box on the calendar for the next day. "Tomorrow is a new day. You can start over again."

Holly looked at today's box. It was X'd out. But the box for the next day was clean. "That sounds good," she said. "I can have a fresh start."

God doesn't want you to carry around your mistakes. When you tell God you're sorry, He forgives you. Just like Holly, you can have a fresh start.

Your Turn

1. Why is it important to tell God that you're sorry for your mistakes?
2. How can you have a fresh start?

Prayer

Lord Jesus, I'm sorry for (name something you're sorry about). Please forgive me. I want to be clean and new. Amen.

Crossing Out My Mistakes

In the left boxes, write mistakes you've made. Then cross them out with an X. In the boxes on the right, draw a picture of a heart to represent Jesus making you new!

God's Ways in Heaven

God's ways are always followed in heaven—it's the home of righteousness!

In keeping with his promise we are looking forward to a new heaven and a new earth, the home of righteousness.

~ 2 Peter 3:13

No Mistakes

Have you ever been to a place where there were no mistakes?

No mistakes means no problems with buildings. No chipped paint, no clogged sinks and no broken light bulbs.

No mistakes means no people problems. Nobody fights, nobody is sick, and nobody gets tired or cranky or hungry.

No mistakes means people don't mess up. There's no burned toast and no bad report cards.

There's just one place like that—where there are no mistakes: heaven!

God fills up heaven with goodness instead of mistakes. Heaven's goodness has a special name. It's called God's righteousness *(right-chuss-ness)*.

God's righteousness is beautiful. That's why when Jacob had a glimpse of the ladder leading to the gate of heaven, he said, "How awesome is this place!" (Genesis 28:17).

God's ways are always followed in heaven. That's why heaven is called the "home of righteousness." God wants us to follow His ways, so we can know some of His goodness now, here on earth.

Your Turn

1. Why are there no mistakes in heaven?
2. Why is heaven so beautiful?
3. How can we know God's goodness here on earth?

_____

_____

_____

Prayer

Father, I pray that I can do things in Your good ways here on earth, just like those good ways are always done in heaven. Amen.

Home of Righteousness

Revelation 21 says that heaven has a Holy City with 12 gates, decorated with jewels. Color the gates to heaven's Holy City!

God Wants Me to Believe

God made a special way for me to be with Him forever.

My Father's will is that everyone who looks to the Son
and believes in him shall have eternal life.

~ John 6:40

Grandma Meets Jesus

Victoria was very sad. Mom had just told her that Grandma had died.

Victoria thought about the fun she always had with Grandma. Grandma would let her dress up in old fancy clothes and play with the collection of fun hats in the hall closet.

Grandma's kitchen was warm and cozy and Grandma made the best peach pie. Victoria loved to curl up in the breakfast nook with Grandma and have a cup of cocoa. Grandma made her feel safe.

"I wish I could be with Grandma forever," Victoria told her mom.

"You can," said Mom. "You just have to wait a little bit."

Victoria thought about how Grandma loved Jesus. Victoria loved Jesus too. She knew she'd be with Grandma again someday in heaven. That made Victoria feel better.

Victoria wanted to be with her Grandma forever. And God wants to be with you forever, too. He's made a special way for that to happen. When you believe in Jesus and tell Jesus you need Him, you'll be with God forever.

Your Turn

1. How does God make it so you can be with Him forever?
2. How can you make sure you'll be with God forever?

Prayer

Lord Jesus, I know I need You. I believe in You. I want to be with You forever. Amen.

With Jesus Forever

On each hat, write the name of a person that you want to be with forever. Pray for each person. Ask God to help them know Jesus and believe in Jesus.

God gives me what I need.

This, then, is how you should pray:
Our Father in heaven,
hallowed be your name,

your kingdom come,
your will be done
on earth as it is in heaven.

Give us today our daily bread.

Forgive us our debts,
as we also have forgiven our debtors.

And lead us not into temptation,
but deliver us from the evil one.

~ Matthew 6:9-13

God is
My Provider

God Meets My Needs

God knows what I need every day and He promises to provide it.

God will meet all your needs according to his glorious riches in Christ Jesus.

~ Philippians 4:19

Jackie's Sneakers

Jackie and her mother were shopping for school clothes. Jackie saw a pair of blue and white sneakers. "These are perfect!" she cried. "Please, Mom, may I have them?"

Mom studied the list they had made together the night before. "I don't see 'new sneakers' here," she said. She looked at Jackie. "Think hard. Are new sneakers a 'need' or a 'want'?"

There's a big difference between what you *need* and what you *want*. Needs are what you must have to live and grow in a healthy way. *Wants* are what you'd like to have, just as extras.

It's easy to get the two mixed up. To check yourself, ask this question: "Is this something I need today in order to live God's way?"

God knows what you need. He promises to give it to you. He will meet your needs every day!

Your Turn

1. Why is it easy to get *needs* and *wants* mixed up?
2. Name a time when you *wanted* something that wasn't a *need*.
3. How does God meet our needs? (Hint: look at today's Bible verse)

_____

_____

_____

_____

_____

_____

Prayer

God, help me to learn the difference between *needs* and *wants*. Amen.

Is It a Need or a Want?

Label each *need* for a healthy life with an "N." Label each *want* with a "W."

- [ ] a safe place to live
- [ ] being first in line
- [ ] eating a healthy lunch
- [ ] knowing Jesus
- [ ] new nail polish
- [ ] people I can love
- [ ] popularity
- [ ] the best spelling grade in the class
- [ ] the chance to learn
- [ ] warm clothes
- [ ] watching my favorite TV show today
- [ ] winning a video game

God Feeds Me

God gives me food to eat for my body and food to eat for my soul.

Jesus declared, "I am the bread of life. He who comes to me will never go hungry, and he who believes in me will never be thirsty."

~ John 6:35

The Last Dollar

Samantha and her mom lived in a small apartment. They didn't have much money, even though Mom worked hard and was careful about spending. One day, Mom said, "We're out of food, Samantha. All I have left is one dollar. Let's pray; I know God will help us."

Mom and Samantha sat at the table. They held hands. "Lord, thank You for my job," Mom prayed. "We have been careful with what You give us. You say You will provide our daily bread. We trust You, God."

Samantha prayed, "God, You have never let us down. Thank You for giving us what we need even before we ask."

There was a knock on the door. Mom got up and opened it. Mrs. Wright, the neighbor upstairs, held two large grocery bags. "I'm going out of town for a week," she said. "I cleaned out my refrigerator. I hope you can use this food, so it won't go bad."

Samantha felt warm inside. God gave them food to eat and He encouraged them, too. He fed their bodies. He fed their hearts.

Your Turn

1. What did Samantha and her mother do when they knew they needed help?
2. How did God feed Samantha and her mother?
3. Why do you think Jesus calls Himself the "Bread of life"?

_____

_____

_____

Prayer

Lord, You are the Bread of life. Thank You for feeding my body and my heart. Help me do my part in getting fed by bringing my needs to You. Amen.

The Bread of Life

Why is Jesus the "Bread of life"? To find out, put the words below in the right order. *Puzzle answers appear at the end of the book.*

TO   HE   THE   AND   FROM   LIFE   DOWN   WORLD
GIVES   COMES   HEAVEN

_____ _____ . . . _____ _____ _____ _____ _____

_____ _____ _____ _____ _____

_____ _____ _____ _____ _____ _____

_____ _____ _____ _____ _____ _____

_____ _____ _____ _____ _____

_____ _____ _____ _____ _____.   *~ John 6:33*

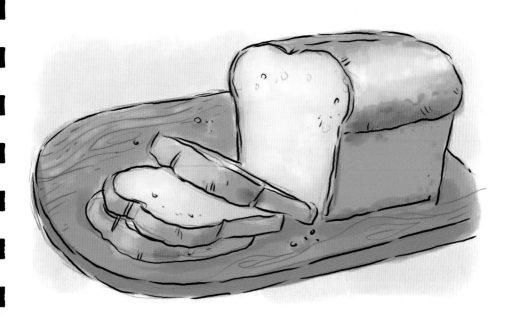

God Gives Me Rest

God provides breaks and rest so I can keep fit.
He makes me lie down in green pastures,
he leads me beside quiet waters.

~ Psalm 23:2

Talia Takes a Break

"Water break!" called Coach Lou. Megan walked to the sideline. She grabbed her water bottle and took a long drink of cool water.

Megan and her teammates sat under a tree. The air was still. Even in the shade, Megan felt drops of sweat trickle down her back. The break felt good. Megan knew she needed rest in order to finish the second half of soccer practice.

But one member of their team was still out on the field. "It looks like Talia doesn't feel well," Megan said to the other girls. Talia put her hands over her eyes. She bent down on one knee.

Megan jumped up and ran to Talia. Coach Lou joined her. "Let's get you out of the sun," he said to Talia. He and Megan helped Talia to the shade.

Megan pressed a cool cloth to Talia's forehead. Coach Lou gave Talia a cup of water. "Give your body a break," he said. "Watch from here during the second half of practice. I need you to be rested for our game on Saturday!"

Talia needed rest. Your body needs rest. God makes sure you have chances to take breaks, get rest and get sleep. Take them!

Your Turn

1. When is it hard to remember to take a break?
2. Why does God want you to get enough rest?

_____

_____

_____

_____

_____

Prayer

God, You provide chances for me get rest. Help me to do my part by taking breaks, getting rest, and getting enough sleep. Amen.

Kinds of Rest

Name the different ways God helps you learn to rest your body.

God Gives Me Strength

**When I put my hope in God,
He will strengthen my body, my heart, and my mind.**
Those who hope in the Lord will renew their strength.
~ Isaiah 40:31

Strength Comes from God

"Ready, set, go!" Mr. Walker, the gym teacher, blew the whistle. The students started the race. They had to run around the track twice.

Taylor breathed hard. She was running out of energy. She needed strength to persist and finish the race.

Jasmine was afraid. She had never run around the track more than once. Could she do it? Jasmine needed strength to try her best.

Aaron didn't feel like running around the track. The sky was blue and the leaves were just beginning to bud on the trees. Why couldn't the class go sit in the grass and stretch instead of running? Aaron needed strength to obey his teacher.

God knows that you need strength from Him to do your best. He can give you all kinds of strength. He can renew your physical energy. He can also give you persistence, confidence, and discipline—strengths in your mind and your heart.

You don't need to find your strength on your own. Put your hope in God. He's got all kinds of strength to give you!

Your Turn

1. What kinds of strength did Taylor, Jasmine and Aaron need?
2. How can you do your part to get connected with God's strength?
3. What promise does God give about strength?

Prayer

God, I need Your strength for (name something you face that is hard). I put my hope in You. Renew my strength, I pray. Amen.

What God's Strength Looks Like

God uses "word pictures" in the Bible to help you understand how He works. A word picture is an example you can see in your mind that explains God.

In Isaiah 40:31, God uses word pictures to describe what happens to people when He gives them strength. Look at the picture below and think of a way God has given you strength!

Those who hope in the Lord will renew their strength.

They will soar on wings like eagles;

they will run and not grow weary,

they will walk and not be faint.

God Gives Me Choices

God lets me choose how I will act.
Turn my heart toward your statutes and not toward selfish gain.
~ Psalm 119:36

Hannah Loses Her Temper

Hannah knew it was wrong to scream at her little brother. But she was angry that he took her new markers. She wanted them back. So Hannah went to Jacob's room and grabbed the markers. "These are *mine!*" she yelled. Then Jacob started to cry.

Roll back the video of Hannah and Jacob in your mind. When Hannah found out that Jacob had taken her markers, she was angry. But at that point, she still had choices. If she stopped for a few moments to think, she could have found another way to get her markers back. For example, she could have politely asked Jacob for her markers. Instead, Hannah chose to lose her temper and do something that she knew was wrong.

You cannot change your feelings, but you have a choice about how you will act. When you have a choice, stop and think about it. There are lots of good ways to act that will honor God. Choose a good way!

Your Turn

1. Name some ways Hannah could have acted differently with Jacob.
2. Why does God allow us to choose how to act?
3. When is it hard for you to stop and think before you act?

_____

_____

_____

_____

_____

Prayer

Lord, You give me choices. You teach me how to act. Help me stop and think so I can make a choice that will please You. Amen.

Choices I Make

Look at the pictures. Write down two choices for each one—one that will please God and one that won't please God.

God Gives Me Friends

God provides me with friends of all shapes and sizes.

Two are better than one.

~ Ecclesiastes 4:9

Avery Moves Away

Julia felt sad. Her best friend, Avery, had moved away on Saturday. Now it was Monday morning and Julia felt all alone.

Julia dragged her feet along the sidewalk to school. She came to the crosswalk. "Good morning, Julia!" said Mrs. Blackwell, the crossing guard, as she gave Julia a hug. "How's my Sunshine Girl today?" Julia smiled. She didn't feel so alone.

Julia got to her classroom a few minutes early. A new girl with braids sat in one of the desks. "Julia, I'm glad you're here," said her teacher. "This is Sonia's first day. Could you show her around the school?" Julia nodded eagerly. She didn't feel so alone.

Later, on the way outside to recess, Julia walked past the basketball court. "Hey, Julia," shouted Tom. "We need another player. Come on." Julia ran onto the court. Tom tossed her the ball. She didn't feel so alone.

No one can take the place of a close friend, but God puts people in your path who you can be friends with. Do what Julia did: be a friend back!

Your Turn

1. Do you think God ever leaves us without any friends at all?
2. Julia learned that she had different kinds of friends. Describe them.
3. What did Julia do to not feel so alone?

Prayer

God, thank You for putting different friends in my life. Help me be a good friend back. Amen.

My Friends

Julia discovered that she has all kinds of different friends. So do you! Your friends can be grown ups, new people, girls and boys your age, or older children. Look at the pictures and think of a friend you have that fits each picture. Pray for each friend you name and thank God for them!

God Gives Healing

God heals my inside hurts and my outside hurts.

I will bring health and healing … I will heal my people and will let them enjoy abundant peace and security.

~ Isaiah 57:18

Serena Falls Down

Serena stumbled into the kitchen. Tears streaked down her cheeks and blood oozed out of her arm.

Mom gave her a hug. "What happened, honey?" she asked, reaching for a warm cloth to help wipe off Serena's cut.

Serena reached down to pull off her shin guards. "I ran into Terrell while I was roller blading," she explained between sniffles. "I fell on the concrete sidewalk. All the boys laughed at me. It was so embarrassing!" She hid her face in her hands.

Serena hurt on the outside...and on the inside.

God understands when you are hurt. He sees your cuts and broken bones. He made every inch of your body, and He promises to give strength to help heal you.

God also understands when you get hurt on the inside. He sees the bruises to your heart. Tell God how you feel. Ask Him to heal you on the inside. He loves you no matter how you feel and no matter what others may say to you. His love can make you whole!

Your Turn

1. What kind of hurt did Serena have on the inside?
2. Name a time when you hurt on the inside.
3. How can you get God's help to heal the hurts in your heart?
4. How does God heal your heart?

_____

_____

_____

Prayer

Lord God, You are the mighty Healer. You can see in my heart that I have been hurt by (name a way your heart has been hurt). You can make me whole. I trust You. Amen.

Hurts in Your Heart

God loves you no matter what. Read each example. Name a heart hurt that goes with it. Put your answers in the heart. Pray about each one so God can heal them!

How I feel when a friend says something unkind.

How I feel when I disobey.

How I feel when I do poorly at an activity.

How I feel when I'm not included.

How I feel when I don't understand.

God Gives Me Courage

God gives me courage to do special tasks for Him.

*Be strong and courageous. Do not be terrified; do not be discouraged,
for the LORD your God will be with you wherever you go.*

~ Joshua 1:9

Haley Prays for Courage

Haley peeked out into the congregation. There were so many people... Oh, why had she said she would light the candles during the worship service?

Pastor Mark put a gentle hand on Haley's shoulder. "Is this your first time lighting the candles?" he asked kindly.

Haley bit her lip and nodded.

Pastor Mark led her to a pair of chairs, and they both sat down. "Look at my hand, Haley," he said. He held his right hand out in front of him. It was shaking!

Haley turned to Pastor Mark, her eyes wide. He smiled. "Yes, Haley. You are not the only one who gets nervous for a big task." He opened up his Bible. "Here's the scripture I read every week before I lead worship: 'Do not be terrified... for the Lord will be with you wherever you go.'"

Haley breathed deeply. "That helps me a lot, Pastor Mark. Thank you."

"It helps me, too, Haley," he said. "How about we pray for each other before the service begins?"

God gave Haley and Pastor Mark each a special task. He helped them do those tasks. God has special tasks He wants you to do for Him. Make sure you ask Him for courage to do the job. He promises He'll be with you and help you.

Your Turn

1. Why do you think Haley and Pastor Mark were nervous?
2. Name a time when you've been nervous before a task.
3. What kind of promise does God give about courage?
4. How can you claim God's promise about courage?

Prayer

Lord God, I want to serve You when You give me a special task, such as (name a job or task). I need Your courage. You have promised to be with me and strengthen me to do the job. I trust You and Your word. Amen.

You Can Be Strong!

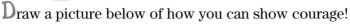

Draw a picture below of how you can show courage!

God Gives Me Special Gifts

I'm good at certain things because God made me that way.
We have different gifts, according to the grace given us.

~ Romans 12:6

Paul's Special Gift

Paul looked at Allison's pumpkin. Allison had painted a colorful face on the pumpkin. "You did a great job!" he said. "How did you learn to paint like that?"

Allison beamed. Paul's compliment made her feel good. "I paint and color all the time," she said.

"You're good at it," said Paul. He turned back to his own pumpkin. He'd painted a crooked mouth and two black circles for the eyes. "I'm not."

"But you're good at something else," said Mrs. Moore, the art teacher, who had just walked over to their table.

Paul was confused. He liked working on art projects, but he never drew or made anything that stood out. "What do you mean?" he asked.

"I believe that Allison can tell you," said Mrs. Moore. "What did Paul do today that was extra special?"

Allison grinned. She turned to Paul. "You told me that you think I'm good at art," she said. "I liked hearing that."

It was Mrs. Moore's turn. "You're very good at bringing out the best in others, Paul," she said.

Paul looked at his pumpkin and then at Allison. "Since you're done with your pumpkin, could you give me some good ideas for mine? Even though Allison is better at art, I have my own special gifts."

Your Turn

1. A "gift" is a special ability. Why do you think God gives each person different gifts?
2. Allison and Paul each had special gifts. What were they?
3. God gives each person gifts. That means He has given some to you! Name a few of the special gifts God has given you. Don't forget to name talents (gifts others can see) and traits (special parts of your personality):

_____

_____

_____

Prayer

God, You created me with special gifts. Help me to learn what they are. Show me how to grow to use my special gifts for You. Amen.

Special Gifts from God

A "gift" can be a talent others can see. It can also be a trait that's a part of your personality. What kinds of gifts do you see in these pictures?

God Gives Me a New Day

Every morning, God gives me a new day and a new chance.

This is the day the LORD has made; let us rejoice and be glad in it.
~ Psalm 118:24

A Change in Attitude

DeSandra just couldn't understand it. Yesterday had been so perfect! She and her brother, Jayden went swimming. Then, they'd had ice cream and played together all day.

But today, Mom asked DeSandra to help hang out the sheets on the clothesline. Then, they picked green beans in the garden. It was sunny and pretty outside, but it was very hot. DeSandra sweated. Mosquitoes bit her. Even when Mom told her to take a break and drink some lemonade, DeSandra felt grumpy.

DeSandra forgot one important thing: her attitude. She'd had fun yesterday with Jayden as they played, but she could have also had a good time with her mom taking care of their house and garden.

Each morning when you wake up, you get a special present from God: a new day!

You can make the choice to be glad about your day or to be mad about your day. How you use each new day is your gift to God. Make it a good one!

Your Turn

1. What did DeSandra forget to notice on the second day?
2. What could DeSandra have done differently on the second day?
3. Why does attitude make a difference in your day?
4. Why does God allow us to choose our attitude?

Prayer

Lord, today You have given me a new day. I will rejoice and be glad in it! Amen.

A New Day

Color the picture of the calendar below and remember that every day is a new day!

Sunday	Monday	Tuesday	Wednesday	Thursday	Friday	Saturday

God forgives me for my mistakes.

This, then, is how you should pray:
Our Father in heaven,
hallowed be your name,

your kingdom come,
your will be done
on earth as it is in heaven.

Give us today our daily bread.

Forgive us our debts,
as we also have forgiven our debtors.

And lead us not into temptation,
but deliver us from the evil one.

~ Matthew 6:9-13

God Forgives Me

God Forgives My Mistakes

**When I ask God to forgive my debts,
I'm asking Him to forgive my mistakes.**

Forgive us our debts.

~ Matthew 6:12

Ming's Debt

"May I borrow a dollar to buy some chips and a drink?" Ming asked her friend, Yan. They were at the refreshment stand at the park. Ming was hungry and thirsty. "I'll pay you back tomorrow at school."

"Sure," said Yan, handing Ming the money. "But please remember to bring it. I have to use that dollar to help pay my library fee."

"Oh, I promise I'll remember," said Ming.

The next morning, Ming saw Yan waiting for her in front of their classroom. "Did you remember to bring the money?" Yan asked.

Oh, no. Ming had forgotten. Yan had been kind to her. Now, Yan would get in trouble because Ming hadn't kept her promise.

Ming had a debt to Yan. Her debt was the money she owed. Ming had made a mistake. She'd forgotten to keep her promise to pay back the debt.

"Please forgive me," she said to Yan.

In the Lord's Prayer, we ask God to "Forgive us our debts." That's a special way of asking God to forgive you for your mistakes. It's like saying, "Lord, I was wrong. I'm in debt to You. Please forgive me."

That's the kind of prayer God loves to hear. He can forgive your "debt" when you tell Him you're sorry for not obeying Him as you should.

Your Turn

1. Why is asking God to forgive your "debts" like asking God to forgive your "mistakes"?
2. Why is asking for forgiveness a prayer God loves to hear?

_____

_____

_____

Prayer

Lord, forgive my debts. Forgive my mistakes. Amen.

Different Ways to Say "Mistakes"

There are different words for your "mistakes" in the Bible. Look at the list. Find the words in the puzzle and circle them. *Puzzle answers appear at the end of the book.*

```
G V D C F A U L T S

T R E S P A S S E S

C V B G V C G I V C

V G T C G V C N G V

M I S T A K E S C G
```

God Knows I'm Not Perfect

Nobody's perfect except Jesus—including me.
*If we claim to be without sin, we deceive ourselves
and the truth is not in us.*

~ 1 John 1:8

Perfect Rebecca?

Rebecca liked being perfect!

She attended Sunday school and church every week, but sometimes during the worship service, she let her mind wander. *I can't stand the dress that Mrs. Woods is wearing*, she thought. But of course, she would never admit thinking things like that. It would mean she wasn't perfect!

Rebecca worked hard at her school work and got good grades. Even so, it made her angry inside that Stephanie got more attention from their teacher than she did. Still, Rebecca didn't admit that she was jealous. It would mean she wasn't perfect.

Rebecca thought she was being God's girl by doing everything right on the outside, but Rebecca made a big mistake: she couldn't admit that she was imperfect.

Rebecca was missing out on God forgiving her and accepting her as she is. God can only forgive people who admit they're not perfect.

Your Turn

1. Why is it easy to think you can be perfect by doing things right on the outside?
2. Is it hard for you to admit you're not perfect? Why or why not?
3. What can you miss out on if you don't admit your mistakes to God?
4. Why can God only forgive you when you admit you're not perfect?

_____

_____

_____

_____

Prayer

Lord, I admit that I'm not perfect. Help me be truthful with You every day. Amen.

News Flash

Fill in the blanks in the newspaper story. Then read it back!

the Daily Paper

November 1st

Girl Admits She's Not Perfect!

Today in _____, a girl named_____,
(your town)   (your name)

age_____, admitted she's not perfect.
(your age)

"This is a wonderful turn of events!" said_____,
(your pastor's name)

her pastor. "It means that_____ can know
(your name)

that God accepts her and forgives her just as she is.

"I know I'm not perfect", said_____. "Only Jesus
(your name)

is. I realized that there's no use to kid myself or anybody

else about it."_____, her family and her church are
(your name)

celebrating God's love for her.

God Knows My Heart

God knows what I'm really thinking and feeling.

The LORD searches every heart and understands
every motive behind the thoughts.

~ 1 Chronicles 28:9

Shauna's Bad Motives

"I'll take Jacob for you, Mom," said Shauna. Her little brother was fussing while Mom tried to sort laundry.

"Are you sure, honey?" Mom raised her eyebrows. It was the first time Shauna had offered to help with her little brother without being asked.

Shauna rolled her eyes. "Yes, Mom, I'm sure."

"Don't let him eat any snacks," said Mom. "It's almost time for dinner."

Shauna took Jacob's hand. They walked downstairs to the kitchen. Then, Shauna opened one of the kitchen cupboards. She found a package of cookies and started eating them.

"Me, cookie too," said Jacob.

"No, Jacob," said Shauna. "Mom said you shouldn't have any snacks before dinner."

"And neither should you," said Mom, standing in the kitchen doorway.

Caught! The main reason Shauna had offered to go downstairs with her brother wasn't to help her mom. She had a different reason—or what the Bible calls a "motive." She wanted to eat cookies even though her mom told her it was almost time for dinner.

God can see in your heart. Ask Him to help you have good motives. If you find out you want to make a choice that doesn't follow God's ways, tell Him. He'll forgive you and help you make a better choice.

Your Turn

1. How did Shauna try to hide her motives from her mom?
2. Did God know why Shauna took Jacob downstairs?
3. Why is it impossible to hide your motives from God?

_____

_____

_____

Prayer

Lord, You see in my heart. Please forgive me for trying to hide my motives from You. Help me make choices that are honest. Amen.

A Peek into My Heart

God looks at your heart all the time. Draw a picture of what He sees there right now.

God Understands "Oops"

I can learn about God from the Bible.
Our help is in the name of the LORD.
~ Psalm 124:8

The New Girl

Riley and Annie walked up the stairs to the church meeting room in the church where they gathered with their scout troop. Another girl climbed the stairs with them. The girl glanced at Riley and Annie. Riley didn't remember seeing the girl before, but she smiled.

Annie didn't say a word or smile to the girl. Instead, she looked away.

The three girls got to the top of the stairs. The mystery girl walked into their troop meeting room with them! Riley was surprised.

"Hi, Tess!" called out two of the other girls.

Riley turned to Annie. "Oops, I didn't know that we have a new girl in our troop," she said. "I feel badly. I should have said hello."

"I knew she was in our troop," said Annie. "She came last week, but I don't think I'm going to like her. I didn't want to say hi, so I didn't."

Neither Riley nor Annie said hello to Tess on the stairs, but each of them had a different reason. Riley hadn't met Tess yet, but Annie made a choice to be unfriendly.

God knows that sometimes you'll have an "oops." You'll make a mistake, but like Riley, it's not on purpose. It's different when you make a choice like Annie's. Her mistake was on purpose. A mistake made on purpose hurts people around you.

When you realize you made a mistake that's an "oops," talk to God. He will show you what to do. He can take your "oops" and turn it around!

Your Turn

1. Why is an "oops" different than a choice?
2. How can God turn an "oops" around?

Prayer

Lord, sometimes I make a mistake that's an "oops." When that happens, help me see the problem and turn it around. And keep me from making mistakes on purpose that end up hurting others. Amen.

On Purpose

Sometimes you don't know you're making a mistake. Sometimes you make mistakes on purpose. Make sure you know the difference. Decide if a mistake was an "oops" or if it was on purpose. *Puzzle answers appear at the end of the book.*

1. Mom tells me it's time for dinner. I don't feel like eating right now so I decide to stay in my room another ten minutes.

    This is an "oops"   This is on purpose

2. My brother's lunch bag and my lunch bag look the same. I'm in a hurry leaving for school and accidentally take his lunch bag on the way out the door.

    This is an "oops"   This is on purpose

3. I'm tired after my bath. I drop my towel on the floor and leave it there. I don't feel like picking it up.

    This is an "oops"   This is on purpose

4. I'm carrying a stack of books for my teacher. I turn the corner in the school hallway and run into Tony and Rick, because I can't see them.

    This is an "oops"   This is on purpose

5. I'm mad at Tammi. She waves to me across the cafeteria. I turn away and don't wave back.

    This is an "oops"   This is on purpose

God Helps Me Turn Around

God helps me turn away from wrong and turn towards right.

Repent! Turn away from all your offenses.

~ Ezekiel 18:30

Kate Gets Lost

"Are you sure you know where you're going?" Danielle asked Kate. The girls were shopping in a big department store. They had gotten separated from Kate's dad, who had been shopping in the toy department.

Kate kept walking. She had to admit it: they were lost, and it was her fault. Dad warned her to stay near him.

Kate remembered what her dad once told her. "If you ever get lost, take a deep breath. Ask God to help you. Then look around for signs."

"Let's stop for a minute," Kate said to Danielle. Kate closed her eyes. She breathed deeply. *God*, she prayed. *I'm sorry I walked away from Dad because I wanted to do my own thing. Right now, we need help.*

Kate looked up. She turned around and studied each sign hanging from the ceiling. "Danielle, we've been going the wrong way," she said, pointing to a sign behind them that said TOYS. The girls turned around and hurried toward Kate's dad.

The same thing happens to you when you tell God you want to turn away from your mistakes. Turning away is called "repentance." Kate told God she was sorry. She asked for help. God showed her what to do. Then, she turned away from going in the wrong direction and went the right way.

That's what repentance is: turning away from doing the wrong thing, deciding to do the right thing, and then acting on it.

Your Turn

1. How do you know when you're doing the wrong thing?
2. What can you do to change direction?
3. Part of repentance is being sorry for doing the wrong thing and turning away from it. What are the other parts?

_____

_____

_____

Prayer

Lord, I'm sorry for (name something you'd like to confess). Please forgive me. I want to repent and turn away from it now. Show me the right way to go. Amen.

The Right Direction

Solve the maze. See what you must do to turn around and go in a different direction to get to Jesus. *Puzzle solutions appear at the end of the book.*

God Wants to Forgive Me

God is happy when I repent and follow Him.

*There will be more rejoicing in heaven over one sinner who repents than
over ninety-nine righteous persons who do not need to repent.*

~ Luke 15:7

Natalie Admits Her Mistake

Natalie's parents insisted that she go to church on Sunday, but Natalie felt horrible. Last week, she had taken some money out of the Sunday school offering. She knew it was wrong. After church, she told her parents. They'd gone with her when she'd taken it back to Pastor Greg.

"I'm so sorry," Natalie had said. "It was wrong. Please forgive me."

Pastor Greg had accepted her apology and was very kind, but Natalie had spent the past six days dreading the morning when she would have to return to the church. Natalie was sure that no one would speak to her at Sunday school.

Natalie and her parents got out of the car and walked into the building. Mrs. Ryan, her teacher, rushed up to her. "I'm glad you're here, Natalie," she said, taking Natalie's hands. "You showed courage last week by admitting your mistake. I'm proud of you!"

Natalie stared. She didn't know what to say.

Miss Stevens, the children's worship leader, hugged Natalie. "Welcome back, Natalie," she said. "We love you." Mrs. Greene, the pianist, put her arm around her and squeezed her. Pastor Greg walked by and gave her a thumbs up.

Did Natalie do the right thing by stealing the money? No, but she did the right thing when she listened to God speaking to her about returning it.

God knows you make mistakes, but when you turn to Him, He forgives you.

Your Turn

1. What mistake did Natalie make? What did she do that was right?
2. How did Natalie's church family show her love?
3. Do you think God stays angry with you after you ask for forgiveness? Why or why not?
4. Why does God rejoice when you say you're sorry?

Prayer

Lord, You rejoice when I ask forgiveness for my mistakes—not because You're happy I got caught, but because You know I'm hearing Your voice. Help me listen to You more and more each day. Amen.

Repentance Party

The Bible says that every time you repent, there's a party in heaven. Color the picture of the Repentance Party. Draw a picture of yourself in the middle of the party.

God Forgives When I Confess

When I confess my sins, God promises to forgive.

If we confess our sins, he is faithful and just and will forgive us our sins and purify us from all unrighteousness.

~ 1 John 1:9

God Sees Everything

Baby Gabrielle screamed. Mama came running. "What happened to the baby?" she asked.

"I don't know," said Maria.

Mama picked up Gabrielle. There was a red mark on the baby's arm. "Maria, do you know anything about this?"

Maria shook her head, but she was lying. She had gotten mad at Gabrielle when the baby had grabbed her hair. Maria had slapped the baby's arm.

Maria was afraid of being punished for hitting her baby sister. She didn't want Mama to know about it, but she kept thinking about what she'd done. She felt badly and she couldn't get it out of her mind.

Mama didn't see Maria hit Gabrielle, but God sees everything. You cannot hide your mistakes from Him.

God promises to forgive you for your mistakes. However, you must first tell Him what you did and that you're sorry. Then He can take away that bad feeling inside. He'll forgive you!

Your Turn

1. What must you do in order for God to forgive your mistakes?
2. Why do you think God wants you to confess your mistakes to Him?
3. How does confessing your mistakes to God make you feel afterward?

_____

_____

_____

_____

_____

Prayer

Lord, I confess that (name a mistake that's been on your mind). I'm sorry. Please forgive me. Amen.

God Sees My Mistakes

God sees all your mistakes, even the ones you may think are hidden. In this picture, there are eight Xs. Each X represents a mistake—and God sees each one. Can you find the Xs? *Puzzle solutions appear at the end of the book.*

God Gives Me a New Heart

I can take off my old heart, and God helps me put on a new one.

Put off your old self...to put on the new self.

~ Ephesians 4:22-24

God Gives Me a New Heart

Ashley tried on sandals for her beach trip. "Look at these pink ones!" she cried. Ashley pulled on the sandals over her old shoes. They didn't look right. They didn't feel right. The sandals didn't work when she still had on her old ones.

"Take off your old shoes first," said Ashley's mom. "Set them aside. Then, put on the new ones."

Ashley took off her old shoes. She put on the pretty, pink sandals. They fit!

You can do the same thing with your heart as Ashley did with her old shoes. When you ask God to forgive your sins, you take off that part of your heart. You put on a new heart—a heart that wants to follow Jesus.

Your old heart and your new heart don't fit well together. Make sure you take off your old heart and turn away from it completely. Then, you can put on your new heart—your heart from Jesus—and it will fit!

Your Turn

1. Why can't you wear two pairs of shoes at once?
2. What can happen to a new pair of shoes when you try to wear them with old ones?
3. Why is it important to decide to turn away from your old way of thinking when you want to be close to God?
4. Why does putting off your old heart make way for your new heart?

_____

_____

_____

_____

Prayer

Lord, I want to be close to You. I choose to put away my old heart. Put a new heart in me and help me follow You. Amen.

Put Off the Old

Find two pairs of shoes in your closet. Put on one pair. Fill in the blanks below and follow the directions as you pray the prayer back to God.

Dear God,

I want to be close to You. I know I've chosen to do things my own way, like (name some times you haven't asked God what to do).

_____

_____

_____

_____

I'm sorry. I want to put off that way of living. (Step out of your shoes and set them aside.)

Please forgive me. I want to follow Jesus. Help me put on a new heart. (Step into the different set of shoes.) Thank You for forgiving me and making me new inside!

Love, _____

(your name)

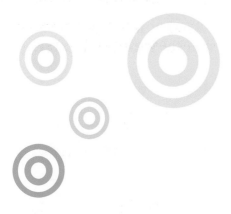

God helps me forgive others.

This, then, is how you should pray:
Our Father in heaven,
hallowed be your name,

your kingdom come,
your will be done
on earth as it is in heaven.

Give us today our daily bread.

Forgive us our debts,
as we also have forgiven our debtors.

And lead us not into temptation,
but deliver us from the evil one.

~ Matthew 6:9-13

God Helps
Me Forgive

I Can Show Forgiveness

I can forgive others because God forgives me.

Forgive as the Lord forgave you.

~ Colossians 3:13

Molly's Mess

The kitchen counter was covered with flour. Sugar crunched under Molly's feet. Pans, spoons and bowls were everywhere.

Molly heard her mother's car pull into the driveway. Uh, oh, thought Molly. Mom is not going to like the mess I've made of her kitchen.

"Molly, what is this?" asked Mom. Her voice shook. Her hands clenched.

"I made brownies," Molly said. "Ben needs to take snacks to preschool tomorrow. You said that you didn't have time to make anything." Molly paused. "I'm sorry about the mess."

Mom took a deep breath. "Thank you, for thinking of others. I forgive you for making this mess. Now finish the job—and clean up!"

Molly sighed with relief. She washed the dishes. She wiped the counters. She swept the floor. Finally, she gathered the trash and took it outside. But when she came back in, she saw crumbs all over the kitchen floor.

Ben ran into the kitchen. "I ate a brownie. It was good!"

Molly was angry. "I just cleaned up. You made a mess!" She pointed to the crumbs on the floor.

Molly's mom forgave Molly's big mess, but Molly didn't want to forgive Ben's little mess.

God reminds us that He forgives all our sins—both our big messes and our little messes. When others need your forgiveness, ask God to help you.

Your Turn

1. Was Molly fair about giving forgiveness? Why or why not?
2. Why is it important to remember how God forgives you?
3. If it's hard to forgive someone, what can you do?

_____

_____

_____

Prayer

Lord, thank You for forgiving my big messes and little messes. Help me forgive others the way You forgive me. Amen.

When I Need Help Forgiving

It can be hard to forgive others. In each set of hands, draw a picture or write down a time when it's been hard for you to forgive. Tell God about each one. Ask Him to help you!

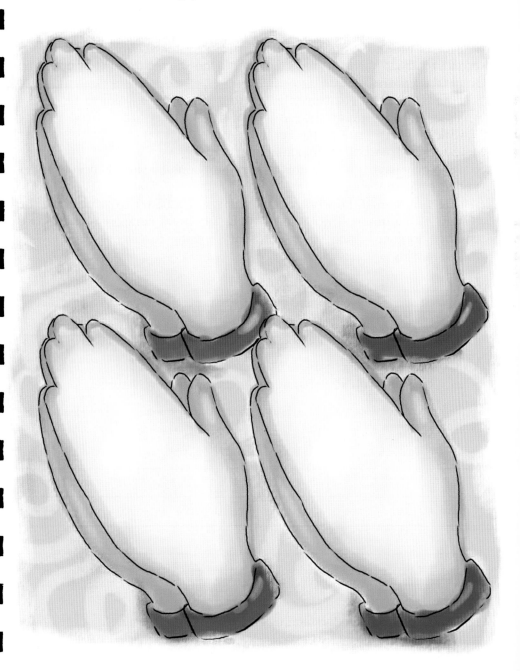

I Can Be Understanding

I can give others the benefit of the doubt and forgive them.

Be kind and compassionate to one another, forgiving each other.

~ Ephesians 4:32

Tasha's Hurt Feelings

Tasha was hurt. Michelle didn't call her after school today like she promised. Was Michelle mad at her? Maybe Michelle didn't want to be friends any more.

But there could be many other reasons why Michelle didn't call.

She may have gotten sick.

She may have had to help her mother.

She may have had too much homework.

She may have not been able to use the phone because her older sister was already on the line.

Tasha assumed the worst about Michelle. It's better to give people the benefit of the doubt. The Bible says, "Be kind and compassionate to one another, forgiving each other." Part of showing forgiveness is showing understanding!

Your Turn

1. Why is it important to show understanding when others make mistakes?
2. Why is showing understanding like showing forgiveness?

_____

_____

_____

Prayer

Lord, help me to be understanding and give people the benefit of the doubt. Amen.

One Reason Why

Try not to think the worst, but give people the benefit of the doubt instead. Name one reason why the person in each situation may be doing what they're doing. Assume the best!

Michael usually stands in the lunch line with me. Today he didn't.
One reason why:

_____

_____

_____

My sister has been hogging the bathroom for twenty minutes, and I can't brush my teeth.
One reason why:

_____

_____

_____

Dad didn't tuck me in to bed tonight.
One reason why:

_____

_____

_____

Mrs. Blake, my teacher, didn't smile at all today.
One reason why:

_____

_____

_____

Justin didn't come to church today.
One reason why:

_____

_____

_____

I Won't Hold a Grudge

God can help me forgive and not hold a grudge.

When you stand praying,
if you hold anything against anyone, forgive him.

~ Mark 11:25

Keisha's Grudge

Keisha's family planned to spend Saturday at the lake park. "We'll take a picnic and go swimming," said Dad.

"Would you like to invite Brandy to go with us?" Mama asked Keisha. Brandy was Keisha's best friend. She lived two houses down the street.

Keisha shook her head. She was mad at Brandy. Last Monday, Brandy invited another girl over to her house to play after school. Keisha wasn't invited.

"I told Brandy she hurt my feelings last week," said Keisha. "She said she was sorry. But I don't forgive her."

Mama nodded slowly. "I see," she said. "Do you plan on being mad at Brandy forever?"

Keisha held a grudge against Brandy. That grudge was like a wall. It stood in the way of Brandy and Keisha having a good time together.

Keisha thought about what Mama said. "I guess forever is a long time to stay mad," she answered. "I'll call Brandy right now."

It's hard to forgive when you are hurt, but when you forgive, you stop feeling angry inside. Don't let a grudge block your way to forgiveness!

Your Turn

1. How does a grudge stand in the way of forgiveness?
2. Do you feel good when you hold a grudge? Why or why not?
3. How can God help you let go of a grudge?

_____

_____

_____

_____

Prayer

God, I confess the times I have held a grudge. I'm sorry. Show me how to forgive others and not hold grudges. Amen.

Get Rid of Grudges

Keisha learned that a grudge was like a wall that kept her from enjoying her friend. Solve the maze. Show Keisha how to get around her grudge and forgive Brandy! *Puzzle solutions appear at the end of the book.*

I Can Get Forgiveness Help

God can help me forgive when others don't understand they've been hurtful.

Jesus said, "Father, forgive them, for they do not know what they are doing."

~ Luke 23:34

Lindsey's Test

Lindsey read the last problem. She closed her eyes and thought hard. All around her, she heard the other students put down their pencils.

"What's taking you so long, dummy?" Seth whispered.

Lindsey tried to ignore Seth. She kept working.

"We'll go out for recess when everyone is finished," said Mrs. Fields. Lindsey looked up. Only one other student was still taking the test.

She looked at the words on the last question once more. She read them slowly. She used the tricks her tutor taught her. She answered the question the best she could. Then, she set down her pencil.

"Please pass your tests forward," said Mrs. Fields. Lindsey reached back and took the stack of papers from Madeline, who sat behind her. "Forget to take your smart pill today, Lindsey?" Madeline jeered.

Those words from Seth and Madeline really hurt me, God, Lindsey prayed to herself.

You may need help forgiving others when they don't understand you. That's a good time to call out to God like Lindsey did and like Jesus did. You can pray, "Help me forgive, God, because others just don't get it." He'll help you!

Your Turn

1. Name a time when others didn't understand you.
2. Is it easy or hard to forgive when you feel misunderstood? Why?
3. Why is God able to understand your hurts, even when others don't?
4. Why is God able to help you forgive others?

Prayer

Lord, help me forgive (name people who have hurt you). They don't know what they are doing. Amen.

Forgiveness Help

When He was on the cross, Jesus said, "Father, forgive them, for they do not know what they are doing." What were some things that people did to Jesus that needed forgiveness? Circle them.

I Won't Judge

I can accept another person's apology just as it is.

You, therefore, have no excuse, you who pass judgment on someone else… you who pass judgment do the same things.

~ Romans 2:1

Amy's Bad Judgment

Amy's teenage brother, Matt, said he was sorry, but Amy didn't believe him.

It was Matt's turn to clean up the bathroom this Friday, but he didn't do it. "It was my friend Bill's birthday," Matt said. "I went to visit him."

Now, it was the weekend. Matt worked all day on Saturday. "I'll clean the bathroom on Saturday evening," he said to Amy. "I promise."

No, thought Amy. Matt is trying to get out of this. He's trying to make me do his chores.

But Amy wasn't able to see into Matt's heart or his mind. Only God understood Matt perfectly. On Saturday night when Amy went to brush her teeth, the bathroom was sparkling! Matt had kept his word. Amy had judged Matt wrongly.

It is not for you to decide if another person is truly sorry. It's important, instead, to listen to that person's apology and accept it as it is. You're not in charge of another person's heart. You're in charge of yours!

Your Turn

1. Was there any way Amy could tell if Matt was being honest or not?
2. Was it Amy's place to decide if Matt was being honest?
3. Why is it impossible to know whether a person is truly sorry or not?

_____

_____

_____

_____

_____

Prayer

Lord, it is not for me to decide if another person is really sorry or not. It's my job to forgive. Help me do that. Amen.

Who Knows?

Solve the rebus to find out who knows a person's heart. *Puzzle solutions appear at the end of the book.*

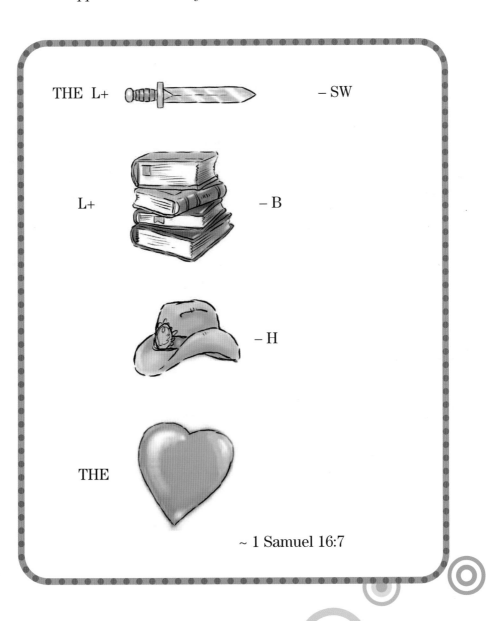

THE L+ [dagger] – SW

L+ [books] – B

[hat] – H

THE [heart]

~ 1 Samuel 16:7

I Can Let Go of Pay Backs

I can learn about God from the Bible.
Our help is in the name of the LORD.

~ Psalm 124:8

The Slumber Party

"I told the other girls that you couldn't come to the slumber party on Friday," Alexis told Tori one morning. "They decided to have the party anyway—without you."

"But I can come on Friday," Tori said. "You gave them the wrong information."

Tori looked away, confused. "You shouldn't have said that," she said. "I wish you would have asked me first." Alexis shrugged and walked away. Her message was clear. Alexis didn't want Tori to go to the slumber party on Friday night.

Tori was angry. Why was Alexis mean to her? Why didn't the other girls ask Tori themselves—didn't they care? Now, Tori was worried that they might be angry with her for not coming. Alexis was to blame. Tori wanted to get back at Alexis. She wanted… revenge.

God, I feel hurt, she prayed. *Alexis was wrong to do this. I want to hurt her back. Help me forgive her. Help me not do something hateful just because I feel badly.*

"Hey, Tori!" said Missy. "I just heard that you can come Friday night after all. What was Alexis thinking? She blew it this time."

Tori smiled. "Yes, I'll be there," she said. *Thank You, Lord*, she prayed.

Your Turn

1. Have you ever wanted to pay back someone when you were hurt?
2. Paying back others can hurt you. Why?
3. Who is in charge of pay backs?
4. How is letting go of pay backs part of forgiveness?

_____

_____

Prayer

God, You are in charge of pay backs. Help me forgive others when they hurt me and leave the rest to You. Amen.

Who Gets Revenge?

Unscramble these words from Romans 12:19 to find out who can get revenge. *Puzzle solutions appear at the end of the book.*

TI   SI   NMEI   OT   NGVAEE

I   LLWI   PYREA   YASS   EHT   RDLO

_____ _____ _____ _____ _____ _____

_____ _____ _____ _____ _____ _____ _____ _____ ;

_____ _____ _____ _____ _____ _____

_____ _____ _____ _____ _____ ,

_____ _____ _____ _____ _____ _____

_____ _____ _____ _____ .

~ *Romans 12:19*

I Can Forgive and Be Free

I can forgive and be free, rather than holding on to unforgiveness.

Blessed are the merciful, for they will be shown mercy.

~ Matthew 5:7

Faith Learns to Forgive

Faith couldn't forget Becca's words. "Why are you eating those cookies and chips?" Becca had said to her loudly one day in the lunchroom. "It's no wonder you're so fat. What a loser."

Faith thought of those words every time she saw Becca. She thought of those words every time she ate her lunch and they made Faith angry inside.

Faith wanted to have better eating habits, but she was afraid. She talked to her mom. "What's the use? I'm a loser when it comes to healthy eating."

"Just because Becca said those words doesn't make them true," said Mom. "You need to forgive Becca."

Faith couldn't believe it. "If I forgive Becca, that's like saying that it was OK for her to talk to me that way!"

"No, Faith," said her Mom. "Forgiving doesn't take away what happened. Forgiving makes *you* free. When you forgive Becca, you're telling God that you don't want to hold that resentment against Becca anymore. You're asking Him to take over!"

Faith bowed her head. "Lord, Becca's words hurt me. But You know the truth. You don't think I'm a loser. You can help me learn better eating habits. I forgive Becca. Please take away my hurt and set me free from resenting her."

Faith learned how forgiveness makes you free. You can learn that, too!

Your Turn

1. Holding onto unforgiveness can hurt you. How did it hurt Faith?
2. Why can it be hard to forgive someone rather than not forgive?
3. Does forgiving mean you say that what a person did is OK?

_____

_____

_____

Prayer

Lord, help me to see when I'm holding on to resentment. Help me let go and forgive. I want to be free! Amen.

Set Free!

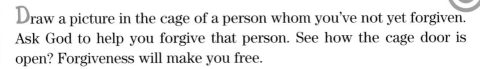

Draw a picture in the cage of a person whom you've not yet forgiven. Ask God to help you forgive that person. See how the cage door is open? Forgiveness will make you free.

I Can Forgive Myself

God helps me learn to forgive myself.
As far as the east is from the west,
so far has he removed our transgressions from us.
~ Psalm 103:12

Sarah's Bad Grade

Sarah stared at the C+ on her spelling test. She'd never gotten a C+ before!

Mrs. Ryan's voice got her attention. "Class, a few of you did poorly on this test. If you want to try and improve your score, you can take this test again tomorrow during the first half of recess, and today's grade can be thrown out." Mrs. Ryan was going to give her another chance!

I don't deserve a second chance, Sarah said to herself. At lunch time, she stopped at Mrs. Ryan's desk. "I want to try again on the test," said Sarah. "But I don't think I deserve it. I don't think I should take it tomorrow."

Mrs. Ryan smiled. "Sarah, I knew when I graded your paper that you had not prepared properly. I'm giving you a second chance because I want to see you do your best." She paused and looked at Sarah. "Forgive yourself and take this chance to try again."

God knows you are not perfect. He knows you make mistakes. He forgives your mistakes.

Your Turn

1. Do you think Mrs. Ryan forgave Sarah for her first test grade? Why or why not?
2. Do you think Sarah forgave herself?
3. God offers you forgiveness, but it can be easy to continue to blame yourself. Why is it hurtful to God when you don't forgive yourself?

_____

_____

_____

Prayer

Lord, You know what's best for me. Help me to trust Your ways and forgive myself. Amen.

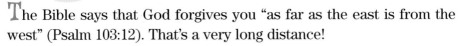

Forgive Me

The Bible says that God forgives you "as far as the east is from the west" (Psalm 103:12). That's a very long distance!

Draw a map below of two places that are a long distance apart. God takes your mistakes away even farther than that. Then think about this: if God can forgive you that much, you can forgive yourself!

I Can Forgive Again

God can help me learn how to forgive over and over.

*How many times shall I forgive my brother
when he sins against me?*

~ Matthew 18:21

I Can Forgive Again

"I'm sorry, I'm late again," said Jenna as she got into the car and shut the door. Mrs. Ernst drove the morning car pool each day.

"No problem, honey," said Mrs. Ernst. "We won't be late. We've allowed extra time."

"Too bad you didn't have time to comb your hair," said Luke. He chuckled. Luke liked to make fun of Jenna and he did a good job of getting her upset every morning.

But today, Jenna didn't answer with a smart remark. Instead, she leaned back in the seat. She thought about how patient Mrs. Ernst was. She looked at Luke. Maybe he didn't understand how annoying his words were. She wanted to be like Mrs. Ernst—not like Luke.

"You know what? You're right, Luke!" Jenna said. She reached into her backpack and took out her comb. She smiled. "I think I'll fix that right now."

Mrs. Ernst laughed. Luke turned red.

Jenna wanted to be forgiving and patient. It wasn't easy with Luke because he teased her over and over, but Jenna found a way. She used a sense of humor to help her forgive Luke.

God can help you find a way to forgive over and over. Ask Him!

Your Turn

1. Why is it hard to forgive the same person over and over?
2. How can God help you forgive someone over and over?
3. Is there ever a time when you shouldn't forgive?

_____

_____

_____

_____

Prayer

God, it's hard to forgive someone over and over, but You've forgiven me over and over. Help me forgive others again and again like You do. Amen.

How Many Times Should I Forgive?

Jesus said we should forgive not just seven times, but 77 times! (Matthew 18:22.) What He meant was that you should be willing to forgive as many times as it takes.

You can draw a Forgiving Tree to show what it means to multiply forgiveness. Start with the heart. Draw two branches. Draw a heart at the end of each branch. Continue to draw two branches off each heart until you fill the page with hearts of forgiveness. That's how much Jesus says to forgive!

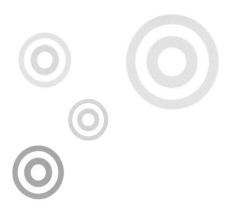

God helps me make good choices.

This, then, is how you should pray:
Our Father in heaven,
hallowed be your name,

your kingdom come,
your will be done
on earth as it is in heaven.

Give us today our daily bread.

Forgive us our debts,
as we also have forgiven our debtors.

And lead us not into temptation,
but deliver us from the evil one.

~ Matthew 6:9-13

God Strengthens Me

I Can Resist Temptation

God helps me resist temptation.

Because he himself suffered when he was tempted,
he is able to help those who are being tempted.

~ Hebrews 2:18

Bethany's Weekend at Grandma's

"Here's your room, Bethany," said Grandma. "I hope you're comfortable." Bethany was spending the weekend at Grandma's house.

There were fresh white lace curtains at the windows and a lovable teddy bear sat in a child's rocker. On the night stand next to the bed were peppermint candies.

"I love it, Grandma!" cried Bethany.

"There's just one thing I need to ask you not to touch," said Grandma. She pointed to the china figurines on the dresser. "Grandpa gave me those china pieces when we first married." Bethany nodded.

"Unpack your things and then come downstairs. I'll fix you a snack," said Grandma.

Bethany looked over at the china figurines. Would it hurt to hold one for just a minute?

God, I want to obey Grandma, Bethany prayed.

"Bethany, I've got crackers and juice ready," Grandma called.

"I'm coming!" said Bethany. *Thank you, God, for helping me walk away from this temptation,* she prayed.

Bethany called to God for help. He answered by helping her get out of a tempting situation. You can call out to God when you face temptation. He'll give you a way to resist!

Your Turn

1. What was Bethany's temptation?
2. What did she do to resist it?
3. How did God help her?

_____

_____

_____

Prayer

Lord, remind me to call out to You for help when I face temptation. You can help me resist. Amen.

When I Call on God

To learn to resist, you need to understand when you're being tempted. Do you know when you need to call on God? Find out by taking the quiz. *Puzzle answers appear at the end of the book.*

I want to do something, even though I know it's wrong.

M I call on God

M I do what I want

I want to do something, even though it would mean disobeying my parents or my teacher.

M I call on God

M I do what I want

I want to do something, even though I'm not sure if it's right or wrong.

M I call on God

M I do what I want

I Can't Blame God, Part I

God can't tempt me because He is totally good.

God cannot be tempted by evil,
nor does he tempt anyone.

~ James 1:13

God is Good

"God tempted me! The chocolate chip cookies smelled so good and no one else was around. I ate a whole dozen." Does God *really* want you to get a stomach ache?

"God tempted me! I saw that my little sister was getting more attention than me, so I got angry and threw my notebook at her." Does God *really* want you to feel left out?

"God tempted me! I didn't understand three problems on the math test, and I could see Tucker's answers so I copied them." Does God *really* want you to cheat?

God doesn't sit on His throne in heaven all day long thinking up ways to tempt you. He doesn't try to make life hard for you and He doesn't try to trip you up.

Instead, God wants you to live the right way. It's wrong to think that God tempts you. He wants only the best for you!

You can't blame God when you feel tempted, because He never tempts anyone. God is pure good, which makes it impossible for Him to try to get you to make a mistake.

Your Turn

1. Why is it easy to think that God tempts you?
2. Why is it impossible for God to tempt you?

Prayer

God, forgive me for blaming You when I'm tempted. You are pure good! Amen.

God's Good Thoughts

God wants good for you, not bad. He does not tempt you. Fill in some good thoughts God has for you. If you need ideas, use some of His promises in the Bible. Remember, God can't tempt you to do wrong things—He can only help you do right things.

I Can't Blame God, Part II

I'm tempted by things I want—not by God.

*Each one is tempted when, by his own evil desire,
he is dragged away and enticed.*

~ James 1:14

The Pink Sweater

Erin saw the pink sweater in the shop window in the mall. She tugged at her mother's sleeve. "Mom, let's go look there!" she begged.

The pink sweater was like a magnet. Erin couldn't keep her eyes off of it. "This is so tempting," said Erin as she stood in front of the store, looking at the sweater.

It didn't matter that she already had 11 sweaters at home in her closet. Instead, Erin imagined what she'd look like in that sweater. She would be so pretty! Erin thought about how the girls in her class would be jealous of her. Lexi and Jordan would demand to know where she got the sweater.

Did God tempt Erin with the sweater? No. God wants Erin to have clothes to wear, but He doesn't want Erin to think only about how she looks.

Erin wanted the other girls to be jealous of her. That was her temptation.

Is it wrong to like pretty things? No. But it's important to understand why you want them.

You can be honest with yourself. You can ask God to help you want things that are really important.

Your Turn

1. Why was Erin tempted by the pink sweater?
2. Would it be fair for Erin to blame God for her temptation?
3. How could Erin learn to face this temptation and get rid of it?
4. Not blaming God means you must look at your own heart.
   Why can that be hard?

_____

_____

_____

_____

Prayer

God, help me be honest and face my temptations. Amen.

What Pulls Me

The pink sweater was like a magnet to Erin—it pulled her in. That's what our temptations do. What "pulls" you? Write down your temptations on the pink sweater. Pray about them. Ask God to help you want things that are really important.

I Can Know Myself

I can stay away from things that tempt me.
Keep your heart on the right path.
~ Proverbs 23:19

Mrs. Hay's Garden

Ella answered the door. Andrew stood there. "Do you want to play?" he asked her.

Ella liked playing outside, but two weeks ago, she and Andrew had gotten into trouble. They had wandered down the road to Mrs. Hay's vegetable garden. "The tomatoes look like red baseballs," said Andrew. "Let's use them to practice our pitching." Ella knew it wasn't right, but it sounded like an adventure. She and Andrew had picked every red tomato and tossed them at the trees behind the garden.

It seemed like fun… until Ella had to apologize to Mrs. Hay's for ruining her nice tomatoes. Plus, she had to work in Mrs. Hay's garden every day for an hour as repayment.

Ella had a good time with Andrew. But when she played with him, she usually got into trouble.

"I don't think I should play with you today," Ella told Andrew. "I've been in enough trouble lately." Andrew turned around and went home.

Ella knew what tempted her. She decided to avoid putting herself in a situation where she could get into trouble. She made a good choice that day to keep herself on the right path!

Your Turn

1. What tempted Ella?
2. Why did Ella tell Andrew she couldn't play?
3. Why is it important to know what tempts you?
4. How can God help you avoid what tempts you?

_____

_____

_____

Prayer

Lord, help me know what tempts me. Please give me strength to avoid it. Amen.

How to Keep on the Right Path

Solve the rebus to find out how to make good choices and avoid temptation. *Puzzle answers appear at the end of the book.*

Your

Proverbs 4:23

___ ___ ___ ___ ___   ___ ___ ___

___ ___ ___ ___ ___ .

~ Proverbs 4:23

I Can Make Good Choices

God helps me make good choices.
You guide me with your counsel.

~ Psalm 73:24

Good and Bad Choices

Some students at Bella's school rode the bus, but Bella didn't need to because she lived just a few blocks away and walked to school.

"Always walk with a friend," her mother told her each morning.

One day, Bella didn't want to walk home with Sam or Sasha or Cody. It wasn't as if something bad had happened. Bella just wanted to feel grown up. She knew she could take care of herself.

Bella picked up her backpack. It felt good to be on her own.

She heard a car behind her. Bella turned to look and the car slowed. There was an adult in the car, but no children. *That's strange*, thought Bella. She felt her heart beat faster. Maybe walking home by herself wasn't such a good idea.

Lord, what should I do? Bella prayed. Then she knew. She turned around and quickly walked back to the school.

"Hey, Bella, where have you been?" shouted Sam. "We've been waiting for you so we could walk home."

That day, Bella made some poor choices and some good choices. She gave in to a temptation when she chose to disobey her mother and walk home by herself. But later, she asked God what to do and she made a good choice by going back to her friends.

Each day you make lots of choices. Always ask God what you should do. He helped Bella make a good choice. And He will help you!

Your Turn

1. Did Bella think carefully about walking home alone?
2. What can get in the way of making good choices?
3. Why is making a poor choice like giving in to temptation?
4. Why does asking God help you make good choices?

_____

_____

_____

Prayer

God, help me make good choices. Remind me to ask You what to do. Amen.

The Best Way to Make Good Choices

Find out the best way to get help making good choices. Color the even numbers yellow. Color the odd numbers purple. *Puzzle solutions appear at the end of the book.*

I Can Find a Way Out

There's always a way to resist temptation.
When you are tempted, he will also provide
a way out so that you can stand up under it.
~ 1 Corinthians 10:13b

Follow the Arrows

Mr. and Mrs. Stowe, Emily's neighbors, had invited Emily and her family to visit their church on Sunday.

"I think I should warn you—our church building is confusing," said Mr. Stowe. "But there's always a way to the sanctuary. Just follow the arrows!"

On Sunday morning, Emily and her family stood outside the church. There were three entrances. "Let's try this one," said Emily's mom.

Inside, there were two hallways and a large staircase. The family started walking. They didn't see anyone.

"Maybe we should just turn around and go home," said Emily.

"No," said her dad. "Mr. Stowe warned us. He said that this would be confusing. He said to look for the arrows."

They came to a new hallway. There were arrows on the wall! Emily and her family turned left, following the arrows. Up ahead, they saw Mr. and Mrs. Stowe. "We found them!" cried Emily.

Mr. Stowe understood that it might be hard for Emily and her family to find their way and so he told them to look for the arrows. God understands that it can be hard for you to make good choices and if you listen to Him, He will help you make the best choice!

Your Turn

1. How did Mr. Stowe help Emily and her family?
2. Why did Emily get discouraged and want to go home?
3. Why can it be hard to know how to make good choices?
4. God makes a promise to help you make choices. What is His promise? (Hint: see today's Bible verse)

Prayer

Lord, You promise that every time I have a choice, You'll show me the way. Help me to look for the way, to see the best choice and to do it! Amen.

The Best Way Out

When you face a temptation or a choice, God promises to show you the best way. Solve the maze to find Emily's best way to the church auditorium. *Puzzle solutions appear at the end of the book.*

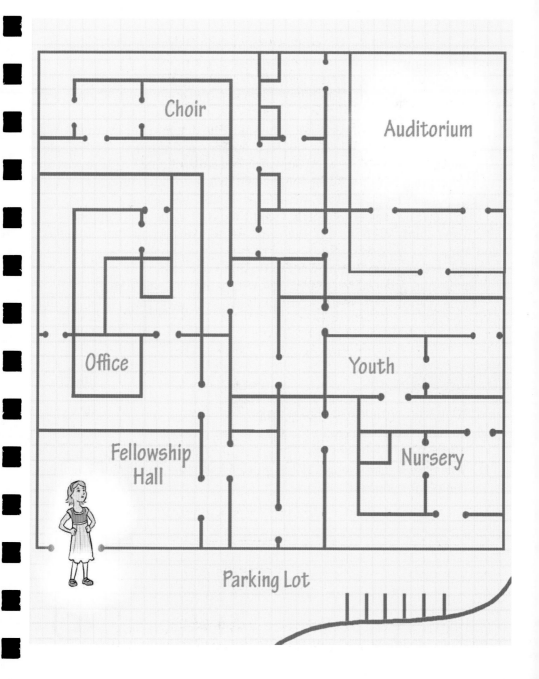

I Can Think for Myself

I don't need to follow the crowd—I can make choices on my own.

Do not follow the crowd in doing wrong.

~ Exodus 23:2

Slumber Party

Nicole, Anna, and Kayla unrolled their sleeping bags in Kayla's bedroom. They had planned this sleepover for two weeks.

Nicole said, "I've got a cool idea. Kayla, where is your phone?"

Kayla was surprised. "Uh, I don't have a phone in my room. There's one downstairs in the den."

Nicole shrugged. "Never mind," she said. She dug into her overnight bag and found her cell phone. She dialed a number and grinned. "Hello," she said, pausing. "Do you know if your refrigerator is running?" There was an answer on the other end. "Well, then, you'd better go catch it!"

Kayla didn't laugh. "Nicole, who did you call?" she asked.

"Oh, don't be concerned Kayla," said Nicole. "I made up a number."

"Wow, think of how fun this will be to call people late tonight," said Anna.

Kayla felt uneasy. "I don't want to do that," she said.

Nicole and Anna stared at her. "Aw, c'mon, Kayla," said Anna.

Kayla shook her head. "No thanks. Let's get that video going instead, OK?"

Your Turn

1. What kind of choice did Kayla make?
2. Would it have been easier for Kayla to just go along with Nicole and Anna? Why or why not?
3. Why does it take strength not to go along with the crowd and to make choices for yourself?

_____

_____

_____

Prayer

Lord, help me know the right thing to do—and then do it. Amen.

Thinking Ahead

You can think ahead and be ready to make good choices. Look at the pictures below. Write down a way you can think for yourself and not go along with the crowd.

I Get Strength from God's Word

I can learn about God from the Bible.
Our help is in the name of the LORD.

~ Psalm 124:8

God's Promise to Ashley

Ashley felt scared and alone. Her best friend, Jessica, was in the hospital.

Ashley thought she should go visit Jessica. "She may not be able to talk with you," Ashley's mother warned. "She has had a serious operation. It will encourage her to see you, but you will have to be strong."

Ashley was tempted not to go. Then, she had an idea. She remembered that Mrs. Donaldson, her Sunday school teacher, had told the class to look for strength from God's Word. She had written down a verse in Joshua which said, "I will never leave you nor forsake you."

"That means God will help me be strong when I go visit Jessica," she thought. "And He is with Jessica, too."

Ashley and her mom bought a "Get Well Soon" balloon and went to the hospital. They found Jessica's room. Jessica looked very tired, but she smiled when she saw Ashley walk into the room.

Ashley sat down next to Jessica. "Jessica, I miss you," she told her friend. "I'm praying for you every day." She took out the piece of yellow paper. "Here is a promise from God." She read Jessica the verse and then put the piece of paper next to Jessica's bed.

Ashley was tempted not to visit Jessica because she was afraid, but God gave her a promise and He strengthened her through His Word!

Your Turn

1. Why did Ashley need strength?
2. What temptation was Ashley trying to resist?
3. How did God's Word help her?
4. What can you do when you need strength from God's Word, but are not sure where to look? (Hint: think about what Ashley did.)

Prayer

Lord, help me find strength from your Word. Amen.

How God's Word Helps Me

Read this verse and underline the different ways God's Word helps you.

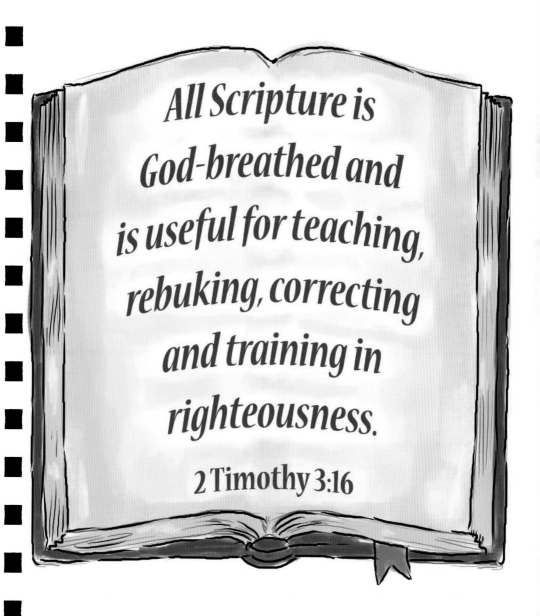

All Scripture is God-breathed and is useful for teaching, rebuking, correcting and training in righteousness.

2 Timothy 3:16

I Can Say Yes to God

God gives me the strength to answer Him and serve Him.

I heard the voice of the Lord saying, "Whom shall I send?
And who will go for us?" And I said, "Here am I. Send me!"

~ Isaiah 6:8

Caitlyn Helps

Caitlyn looked at the big stack of flyers. "Will you go walk with me?" asked Mrs. Martin, one of the leaders of the after-school Sonshine Club. "I need to pass out these flyers in the neighborhood across from the church."

Caitlyn knew the flyers were important. The flyers announced the church's Easter party and egg hunt where parents and children would play games, have snacks, and hear the Easter story.

Caitlyn had plenty of free time. She had already finished her homework and didn't have anything else to do today at Sonshine Club.

I know that the flyers are important, and I have nothing else to do right now. So why do I feel nervous about passing out flyers? Caitlin wondered.

"I know you've never done this before, Caitlyn," said Mrs. Martin. "But I'll be with you. Please say yes!"

Caitlyn smiled at her friend. "It's true, I feel weird because this is something different for me," said Caitlyn. "But I'll go with you. I'll help you!"

Caitlyn thought carefully about why she should help. It would have been easier for her to stay with her friends at Sonshine Club and play, but she was willing to try something different to serve God.

God works through people. He will call you to do special things for Him. You can be ready to do your part for God. When the time comes, you can say yes to God!

Your Turn

1. Caitlyn didn't answer Mrs. Martin right away. Why?
2. Why can it be hard to try something different?
3. How can you be ready to say yes to God?

_____

_____

_____

_____

Prayer

Lord, here I am. Use me! Amen.

People God Uses

These people were tempted to say no to God, but then said yes. Draw a line to match up each person's name with the correct description. *Puzzle solutions appear at the end of the book.*

A boy with a slingshot who killed a giant	Ruth
A young woman who moved to a new country to be loyal to her family	Peter
A young girl who gave birth to Jesus	David
A fisherman who started the church	Mary

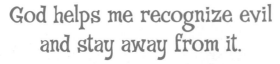

God helps me recognize evil and stay away from it.

This, then, is how you should pray:
Our Father in heaven,
hallowed be your name,

your kingdom come,
your will be done
on earth as it is in heaven.

Give us today our daily bread.

Forgive us our debts,
as we also have forgiven our debtors.

And lead us not into temptation,
but deliver us from the evil one.

~ Matthew 6:9-13

God Protects Me

God is Stronger Than Evil

**I can count on God's goodness to be greater
than any bad evil in the world.**

The one who is in you is greater than the one who is in the world.

~ 1 John 4:4

Look for God's Goodness

Elizabeth walked out to the driveway to collect the paper. She looked at the front page. There was a picture of three young children. They were sad. They wore rags and looked very dirty.

Elizabeth ran inside. "Mom, what happened to these kids?" she asked, pointing to the picture. Together, Elizabeth and her mother read the story. They found out that the three children had lost their parents because of a war in their country.

"Look, Elizabeth," said Mom. "You missed this part. There are relief workers helping the children. The workers are trying to find them a new home." Elizabeth saw a lady and a man standing behind the children.

"What happened to these children is very bad," said Elizabeth.

Her mother nodded. "Yes, that is true. There is evil in this world." Mom paused. "But God is using these workers to show us His goodness!"

God is good. God worked through the relief workers to help the three children. He can work through you to help other people see His goodness. Look for God's goodness every day. Ask Him to help you see it and He'll show you!

Your Turn

1. Name an evil you see in the world.
2. Name a way you see God working His good in the world.
3. How can you see God's goodness in the world every day?

_____

_____

_____

_____

Prayer

God, show me Your goodness around me today. Amen.

Seeing God's Goodness

Lots of people focus on bad things. With practice, you can focus on seeing God's goodness instead. Think back over the past day. Write or draw a picture of how you saw God's goodness working through other people in your world.

God Has an Enemy

God is good but He has an enemy who is bad.
(Train yourselves) to distinguish good from evil.
~ Hebrews 5:14

The Revolt Against God

Since God is so good, it can be hard to understand that He has an enemy. But He does.

God's enemy is named Satan. Satan used to be God's friend. In fact, Satan was an angel.

Satan decided that he was just as good as God. Satan wanted to be the boss. He wanted to do things his own way.

But only God can rule in heaven. Plus, God is stronger than anyone or anything. Since Satan disobeyed God, he got kicked out of heaven! That made Satan even madder. He didn't stop trying to be better than God. Instead, he made matters worse.

Satan got other angels to join him against God. He took a whole lot of angels with him when he got kicked out of heaven—one third of them! You can read more about how it happened in Isaiah 14:12-15 and Revelation 12:3-4.

Satan is still fighting against God. You can't see him because he is a spiritual being, just like God is a spiritual being. The Bible tells us that Satan tries to get people to come to his side. Don't let him. Say yes to God—because God is good. Satan isn't.

Your Turn

1. Is it hard for you to understand why Satan would be against God? Why or why not?
2. Do you think evil is a real thing?
3. God is stronger than Satan. How does that make you feel?

_____

_____

_____

_____

Prayer

Lord God, You are good and strong. I want to be on Your side. Amen.

Opposites

God and Satan are opposites. God is good. Satan is bad. Both God and Satan have lots of different names in the Bible. Sort the list below. Put God's names on one list and Satan's on the other. *Puzzle solutions appear at the end of the book.*

<u>GOD</u>   <u>SATAN</u>

devil

enemy

Friend

father of lies

Holy One

evil one

Good

Light

prince of darkness

Savior

Truth

wicked one

God Has Won

Jesus has won the fight of good over bad.
*Thanks be to God! He gives us the victory through
our Lord Jesus Christ.*

~ 1 Corinthians 15:57

Janelle's Big Win

"One more game?" Uncle Bill asked Janelle, as he sorted the red checkers from the black checkers.

Janelle yawned. She was tired. "I'm not sure," she said. "Plus, I beat you three games to one already."

"All the more reason for you to want to play," said Uncle Bill. "Remember, we agreed that the best of five wins. You can't lose!" Even if Janelle lost the last game, she still would win the entire match over Uncle Bill, three games to two.

Janelle had already won. The same is true with Jesus. He has already won the battle of good over bad. When Jesus went to the cross, He took the blame for everybody's mistakes—even yours. But taking the blame didn't keep Jesus down. He beat death. He rose again. His friends saw Him, spoke with Him, walked with Him and ate with Him. He won!

When you choose to live for Jesus, you have nothing to lose. He's already won the fight between right and wrong. You can trust Him to help you and deliver you from the evil one. Jesus has beaten the bad guys. He'll help you live for Him!

Your Turn

1. How has Jesus already won the fight of good against bad?

2. Why can you trust Him to help you?

_____

_____

_____

_____

_____

_____

Prayer

Lord, I praise You. Jesus has won the fight of good over bad. Amen.

Victory!

F ill in the Victory Announcement!

Proclamation

Let it be known that Jesus Christ, the Son of God, has won the fight of good over bad!

This victory is seen in_____
(name something good you've seen)

and_____
(name something else good you've seen)

Let it be known that _____ is on
(your name)

Jesus Christ's side in the battle and she will

share His victory!

Signed on_____
(today's date)

God Sees What's True

I can recognize evil and avoid it.
Satan himself masquerades as an angel of light.
~ 2 Corinthians 11:14

Rachel's Costume Party

Rachel smoothed the blue folds of her dress. She shifted her baby doll from one hand to the other. The costume party was about to begin. Children were told to come dressed up as characters from Bible times. Rachel was dressed as Mary. She carried the "Baby Jesus" with her.

Rachel saw shepherds, warriors, and kings. One girl was dressed as Queen Esther. Then, the door to the ministry building opened. A stunning angel walked inside.

Rachel stared. White, sparkles, glitter—the angel was beautiful!

"Who is dressed as the angel?" Rachel asked her friend, Erin.

Erin frowned. "You're not going to believe it," she said. "I think it's Jessica. You know, the class bully."

"Why would the class bully dress as an angel?" Rachel wondered.

"To get people to like her," said Erin. "To get them to come to her side."

That's exactly what God tells us happens with evil. Satan tries to trick you into thinking his way is good. He wants you to see things his way. Satan "dresses up" his bad plans to make them look appealing.

Don't let Satan fool you. He's a master at making choices seem confusing to you. But God sees the truth. You can have God's wisdom to see things the way they really are. Ask God to show you what is true and real.

Your Turn

1. Why does Satan want to confuse you?
2. Why does Satan "dress up" your choices?
3. How does God help you see through Satan's tricks?

_____

_____

_____

Prayer

Lord, deliver me from being tricked by Satan. Help me make good choices based on Your truth. Amen.

The Hidden Truth

One way Satan tries to trick you is by keeping you from reading your Bible. He wants you to think you can't understand it. Don't let Satan keep you from reading your Bible and getting closer to God. Circle the five Bibles hidden in the picture. Make sure you know where your own Bible is and be sure to read it every day! *Puzzle solutions appear at the end of the book.*

God Helps Me Be Alert

I need to be alert and watch for danger.

Be self-controlled and alert. Your enemy the devil prowls around like a roaring lion.

~ 1 Peter 5:8

Lacy Visits the Zoo

Lacy and her home school group were visiting the zoo. They stood at the lion's cage. It was feeding time.

Lacy studied the signs on the outside of the cage. They read, *Stand back. Do not feed the lions. Do not place objects inside the cage.*

The largest lion was hungry. He stood up. He paced back and forth. He licked his lips. Lacy saw the lion's sharp teeth.

Then, the lion saw the zoo keeper near the fence with a bucket. The lion roared! Food was on the way.

"I'm glad the zoo keeper finally got here with food," Philip said to Lacy. "The lion could be dangerous to us."

Lacy nodded. "I'm glad we saw the rules and obeyed them."

The Bible tells us to be aware of danger. In fact, the Bible says that danger can come from God's enemy, Satan, who acts like a lion. You could say he "prowls" like a lion because he's sneaky. He likes to discourage you. He likes to make you think that God doesn't care.

Be watchful. Ask God to help you know when the danger of evil is nearby. God will help you recognize danger. He will help you resist it.

Your Turn

1. Why did Philip and Lacy think the lion could be dangerous?
2. How did they do their part to be aware of danger?
3. In what ways is Satan like a lion?
4. How can you be prepared for danger?

_____

_____

_____

Prayer

God, make me aware of the dangers around me. Show me how to do my part to resist them. Amen.

On The Prowl

The Bible compares Satan to an animal. Connect the dots to find out which animal it is. *Puzzle solutions appear at the end of the book.*

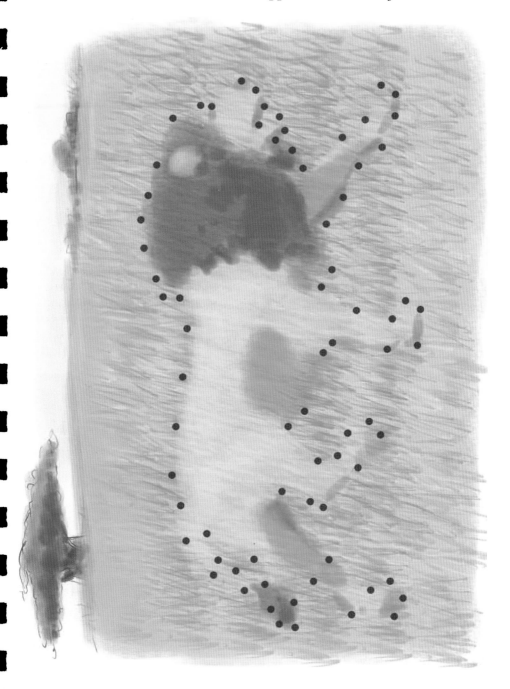

God Gives Hope

**I can hope in God, even when my heart,
my mind or feelings get hurt.**

All-surpassing power is from God and not from us.

~ 2 Corinthians 4:7

Justine Faces Her Fears

"Come on, Justine," said Carrie. "I know you don't like the playground slide. But we'll be right there at the bottom, waiting for you. Won't we, Sara?" Sara nodded. Both girls tried not to giggle.

Justine looked at Carrie and Sara. She wanted them to like her. She wanted to be friends with them, but she was afraid of the slide. It was high, and she didn't like being up off the ground.

"You can do it, Justine," said Sara. "Go ahead." The girls led Justine around to the slide's steps. They watched while she climbed up.

One, two, three... Justine held on tightly to the rail as she climbed. Soon, she was at the top. She looked down. "Carrie! Sara! Here I come!"

Carrie and Sara pointed and laughed. "Scaredy cat!" they called and ran away.

Justine felt weak. Her hands started to shake. Carrie and Sara had left her.

I'm not alone and I won't give in, thought Justine. *I know God is with me. I can count on Him.* She sat at the top of the slide. She prayed once more and then slid down. At the bottom, her feet touched the ground. Justine smiled. God helped her be strong.

You can call on God because God is powerful enough to protect you in any situation.

Your Turn

1. How was Justine hurt?
2. Why did she call on God?
3. Have you ever had your heart or your feelings hurt?
4. How do you know you can count on God to give you hope, even when your heart hurts? (Hint: see today's Bible verse)

Prayer

God, You can give me strength even when I hurt inside. Remind me to call on You, my God of hope! Amen.

A Time for Hope

Draw a picture or write down a time when you were pressured, confused, made fun of, or put down. Pray about your heart and your feelings. Ask the God of hope to show you how to forgive, be healed, and be strong!

We are hard pressed on every side, but not crushed; perplexed,
but not in despair; persecuted, but not abandoned;
struck down, but not destroyed.

~ 2 Corinthians 4:8-9

God's Word Helps Me

God's Word protects me and helps me be strong when I'm afraid.

The word of God lives in you, and you have overcome the evil one.

~ 1 John 2:14

The Big Storm

Bright lightning lit up the sky. Thunder roared. Winds blew down tree branches, and rain poured down.

Abigail was scared. The storm had lasted since dinner. Now it was bedtime, and Abigail was afraid to go to sleep.

"I have an idea that may help calm your fears," said Dad. He opened the Bible. He read, "Jesus said, 'Peace I leave with you; my peace I give you… Do not let your hearts be troubled and do not be afraid.' That's from John 14:27."

Abigail thought about Jesus. She remembered a story from Sunday school. Jesus was so calm during a storm that He fell asleep in a boat. "Do you think Jesus wants me not to be afraid?" she asked her father.

"Oh, yes," said Dad. "In this verse, you heard how He wants you to have peace. You can do your part to take Him at His word."

Abigail shut her eyes. She thought about Jesus' words. She fell asleep.

God's Word is powerful. When you read it, think about it, and accept its truth, then God works through you to strengthen you. God protects you with His Word!

Your Turn

1. What did Abigail do when her father read Jesus' words?
2. How did God's Word help calm Abigail?
3. Why is God's Word so powerful?

_____

_____

_____

Prayer

Thank You, God, for making plans to care for me. Thank You for Your Word. Help me to read it, think about it, and accept its truth. Amen.

My Heart Box

The Bible says to "Lay up his words in your heart" (Job 22:22). Make this Heart Box to hold your favorite verses from God's Word.

What you need:

1. a small empty box, such as a Jell-O box, pudding box or bottom half of a macaroni and cheese box
2. gift wrap paper
3. clear tape
4. construction paper
5. glue stick
6. scissors
7. index cards
8. pen or pencil

What to do:

Trim the top flaps of the box. Cover the box with gift wrap paper, folding the top edges to the inside of the top of the box. Tape into place.

Cut out two hearts from construction paper. With a glue stick, attach hearts onto the front and back of the box.

Use the index cards to record your favorite Bible verses, either from this book or from your own reading. Place the cards in the box.

Keep your Heart Box in a special place. Re-read your favorite verses every day to help you memorize them. Add more verses on extra index cards whenever you like!

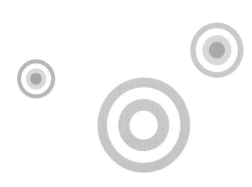

God Wants Me to Ask

I can ask God for help to protect me.
*I call to the LORD, who is worthy of praise,
and I am saved from my enemies.*

~ Psalm 18:3

Erica's New Neighborhood

Erica's lip trembled. She watched as her older brother Mitchell raced ahead of her on his bike.

Erica and Mitchell had just moved to the neighborhood. Erica felt confused about where to ride, but Mitchell was confident.

Erica stopped pedaling. Tears filled her eyes. She didn't know where to go. She could barely see Mitchell. "Mitch," she called out. "Where are you? Help!"

Mitchell heard her. He turned around and pedaled back. "You look upset, Erica," he said. "Why?"

"I don't want to get lost," she said. "I thought you were leaving me."

Her big brother gently punched her shoulder. "No way!" he said. "I'm glad you called out to me for help. Otherwise, I'd be in trouble with you and Mom."

Erica didn't have to be strong all on her own. Her brother never left her, even though she thought he did.

It's easy to forget to ask for help. The Bible says, "You do not have, because you do not ask God" (James 4:2). God is always near you. He protects you. Call out to Him when you feel danger or confusion. He'll let you know that He's with you!

Your Turn

1. What can keep you from asking God for help?
2. Why does God want you to ask Him for help?
3. What does God promise when you ask Him for help?

Prayer

Lord, remind me to ask You for help when I'm afraid, when I'm in danger, and when I need protection. Amen.

Sing a Reminder

The Bible says we forget to ask God for help. He's there all the time to give it! Here's an simple song you can learn to remind you to ask God for help.

Sing these words to the tune of *Row, Row, Row Your Boat*. They're easy to remember!

> Ask, ask, ask for help
>
> Ask our God for help
>
> Ask, ask, ask for help
>
> Ask our God for help.

God Protects Me Forever

I can be sure I'll be with Jesus forever because of God's promises.

Everyone who calls on the name of the Lord will be saved.
~ Romans 10:13

God Protects Me Forever

Jesus taught His disciples to pray, "Deliver us from the evil one" (Matthew 6:13). There are different times you need God's protection.

You need His protection during your day to help you be safe and make good choices.

You need His protection when you're thinking about things. God helps you see the truth.

You need His protection to live out His love and hope, rather than letting discouragement and dislike rule in your heart.

You need His protection forever, so that you can be with Him in heaven.

God's protection isn't something you can make on your own, like a craft or a cake. It's something that comes from Him when you ask.

It's simple to get God's protection forever. The Bible says, "Everyone who calls on the name of the Lord will be saved" (Romans 10:13). When you do that, He promises you'll be with Him forever.

Your Turn

1. Name some different times when God protects you.
2. How can God protect you forever?
3. Tell God you want to be with Him forever!

_____

_____

_____

_____

_____

Prayer

Lord, I know I need Your protection. I want to be with You forever. I call on You and ask You to save me. Amen.

When I Call on God

What happens when we call on God's name and tell Him we need Him? Substitute the numbers with the letter in the key to find out. *Puzzle solutions appear at the end of the book.*

1=B	5=H	9=R
2=D	6=I	10=T
3=E	7=L	11=V
4=F	8=O	12=W

___ ___ ___ ___ ___ ___ ___ ___
12 3   12 6 7   7   1   3

___ ___ ___ ___ ___ ___ ___
12 6   10 5   10 5   3

___ ___ ___ ___
7   8   9   2

___ ___ ___ ___ ___ ___ ___.   ~ 1 Thessalonians 4:17
4   8   9   3   11 3   9

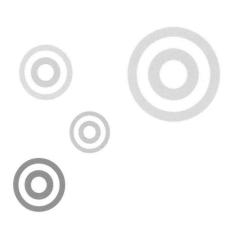

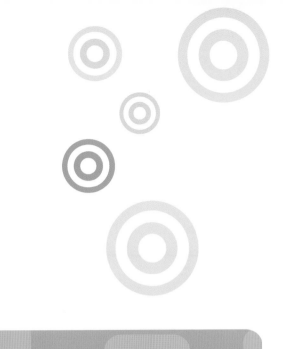

Index of Scripture References

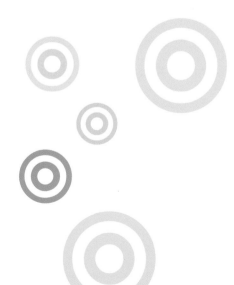

Index of Scripture References

Psalm 118:24	God is my Provider, God gives me a new day
Psalm 119:28	God strengthens me, I get strength from God's Word
Psalm 119:36	God is my Provider, God gives me choices
Psalm 145:18	God is my Friend, I'm always near God
Psalm 149:4	God is my King, My King enjoys me
Proverbs 18:10	God's names, God's good names
Proverbs 23:19	God strengthens me, I can know myself
Ecclesiastes 4:9	God is my Provider, God gives me friends
Isaiah 6:8	God strengthens me, I can say yes to God
Isaiah 40:25	God's names, God is the Holy One
Isaiah 40:31	God is my Provider, God gives me strength
Isaiah 55:9	God's ways, God's ways are best
Isaiah 57:15	God is my King, My King lives in me
Isaiah 57:18	God is my Provider, God gives healing
Isaiah 64:8	God is my heavenly Father, God is our Father
Jeremiah 29:12	God is my Friend, I can count on God to listen
Jeremiah 33:3	God is my Friend, I can call God anytime
Ezekiel 18:30	God forgives me, God helps turn me around
Daniel 2:44	God is alive, Heaven is a safe place
Matthew 1:23	God's names, God is Immanuel
Matthew 3:3	God is my King, My King is coming
Matthew 5:7	God helps me forgive, I can forgive and be free
Matthew 6:9	God is my Friend, I can pray like Jesus

Matthew 6:12	God forgives me, God forgives my mistakes
Matthew 6:33	God is my King, My King comes first
Matthew 15:18	God is my Friend, I can be myself with God
Matthew 18:21	God helps me forgive, I can forgive again
Mark 11:25	God helps me forgive, I won't hold a grudge
Luke 10:20	God is alive, Jesus' special book
Luke 11:1	God is my Friend, I can pray with others
Luke 15:7	God forgives me, God wants to forgive me
Luke 18:1	God is my Friend, I can keep praying
Luke 19:11	God is my King, My King is good
Luke 23:24	God helps me forgive, I can get forgiveness help
John 4:24	God's names, God is Spirit
John 6:35	God is my Provider, God feeds me
John 6:40	God's ways, God wants me to believe
John 8:12	God's names, God is my Light
John 10:29	God is my heavenly Father, God is the best
John 13:13	God's names, God is my Teacher
John 13:35	God is my King, My King loves through me
John 14:2	God is alive, Heaven has room for me
John 14:3	God is alive, Jesus is always with me
John 14:4	God is alive, Heaven is a real place
John 14:16-17	God is alive, Jesus sends the Holy Spirit
John 15:15	God is my Friend, I can talk to God

Acts 1:9	God is alive, Jesus is alive
Acts 7:55	God is alive, Jesus is God's right hand Man
Romans 2:1	God helps me forgive, I won't judge
Romans 8:26	God is my Friend, I can get prayer help
Romans 10:13	God protects me, God protects me forever
Romans 12:6	God is my Provider, God gives me special gifts
Romans 12:19	God helps me forgive, I can let go of pay backs
1 Corinthians 10:13b	God strengthens me, I can find a way out
1 Corinthians 15:57	God protects me, God has won
2 Corinthians 4:7	God protects me, God gives hope
2 Corinthians 5:17	God's ways, God makes me new
2 Corinthians 6:18	God is my heavenly Father, God calls Himself "Father"
2 Corinthians 11:14	God protects me, God sees what's true
Galatians 2:20	God is alive, Jesus lives in me
Galatians 4:6	God is my heavenly Father, God is my heavenly daddy
Ephesians 1:9	God's ways, God tells me His ways
Ephesians 2:10	God's ways, God wants me to help
Ephesians 4:22-24	God forgives me, God makes my heart new
Ephesians 4:32	God helps me forgive, I can be understanding
Ephesians 6:18	God is my Friend, I can listen to God
Philippians 2:10	God's names, God's name is honored
Philippians 4:13	God's ways, God helps me
Philippians 4:19	God is my Provider, God meets my needs

Colossians 3:13	God helps me forgive, I can show forgiveness
1 Thessalonians 5:18	God's ways, God wants me to be thankful
2 Timothy 2:19	God is my heavenly Father, God knows me
James 5:16	God is my King, My King answers prayer
1 Peter 2:15	God's ways, God wants me to do good
1 Peter 5:7	God is my heavenly Father, God cares
1 Peter 5:8	God protects me, God helps me be alert
2 Peter 3:13	God's ways, God's ways in heaven
1 John 1:8	God forgives me, God knows I'm not perfect
1 John 1:9	God forgives me, God forgives when I confess
Hebrews 2:18	God strengthens me, I can resist temptation
Hebrews 5:14	God protects me, God has an enemy
James 1:13	God strengthens me, I can't blame God, Part I
James 1:14	God strengthens me, I can't blame God, Part II
1 John 2:14	God protects me, God's Word helps me
1 John 4:4	God protects me, God is stronger than evil
Revelation 22:20	God is my King, My King needs an invitation

Puzzle Answers

Page 17
PRAYERS THAT DON'T KID
Answer:
FROM THE HEART

Page 27
ONE WAY TO PRACTICE PRAYING
Answer:
PRAY CONTINUALLY

Page 39
GOD'S HANDS OF POWER
Answer:
Psalm 16:8: Girl on balance beam
Psalm 17:7: Girl praying
Psalm 60:5: Girl on the ground

Page 41
MY GOD SHIELD
Answer:

Page 55
HOW LONG DOES THE HOLY SPIRIT
LIVE?
Answer:
FOREVER!

Page 59
WITH YOU FOREVER
Answer:

```
J B X T O K A I
D W G J F S B T
E Y R S M I R L
U J O S A J Q U
L E H P C E I P
V S L E N S G H
A Q U S Z U D C
A U S W I S P V
Z P E J K Y U B
F N J T X R A O
C O Y Q V W Z D
W B S U S E R I
```

Page 65
GOD'S HOME
Answer:

Page 67
TRIP TO HEAVEN
Answer:

Page 77
HOW TO BE PERFECT?
Answer:
I'm not perfect but the
H O L Y   O N E
can change me!

Page 79
ALWAYS WITH US
Answer:
Jesus said,
"I am always with you."
Matthew 28:20

Page 87
FIND THE LOST SHEEP
Answer:

PAGE 115
STRAIGHT PATHS TO GOD'S
KINGDOM
Answer:

Page 119
PLANS PUZZLE
Answer:

```
Z  X  Z  X  X  Z  Z  X
P  U  R  P  O  S  E  S
X  W  I  L  L  Z  X  Z
Z  X  Z  A  Z  X  Z  X
X  Z  X  N  X  Z  X  Z
W  A  Y  S  Z  X  Z  X
```

Page 121
THE WAY THAT WORKS
Answer:

Page 123
THE RIGHT WAY
Answer:
TEACH ME TO DO YOUR WILL.
~ Psalm 143:10

Page 141
THE BREAD OF LIFE
Answer:
He...comes down from heaven and gives life to the world.
~ John 6:33

Page 161
DIFFERENT WAYS TO SAY "MISTAKES"
Answer:

```
G  V  D  C  F  A  U  L  T  S
T  R  E  S  P  A  S  S  E  S
C  V  B  G  V  C  G  I  V  C
V  G  T  C  G  V  C  N  G  V
M  I  S  T  A  K  E  S  C  G
```

Page 167
ON PURPOSE
Answer:
1. This is on purpose
2. This is an "oops"
3. This is on purpose
4. This is an "oops"
5. This is on purpose

Page 169
THE RIGHT DIRECTION
Answer:

Page 173
GOD SEES MY MISTAKES
Answer:

Page 183
GET RID OF GRUDGES
Answer:

Page 187
WHO KNOWS?
Answer:
The Lord looks at the heart.

Page 189
WHO GETS REVENGE?
Answer:
It is mine to avenge; I will repay, says
the Lord.

Page 199
WHEN I CALL ON GOD
Answer:
"I call on God" for all three questions.

Page 205
HOW TO KEEP ON THE RIGHT PATH
Answer:
Guard your heart.
~ Proverbs 4:23

Page 207
THE BEST WAY TO MAKE
GOOD CHOICES
Answer:

Page 209
THE BEST WAY OUT
Answer:

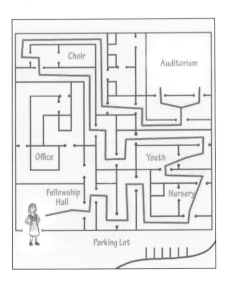

Page 215
PEOPLE GOD USES
Answer:
A boy with a slingshot who killed a giant – David

A young woman who moved to a new country to be loyal to her family– Ruth

A young girl who gave birth to our King – Mary

A fisherman who started the church– Peter

Page 221
OPPOSITES
Answer:

God	Satan
Friend	devil
Good	evil one
Holy One	enemy
Light	father of lies
Savior	prince of darkness
Truth	wicked one

Page 225
THE HIDDEN TRUTH
Answer:

Page 227
ON THE PROWL
Answer:

Page 235
WHEN I CALL ON GOD
Answer:
We will be with the Lord forever.

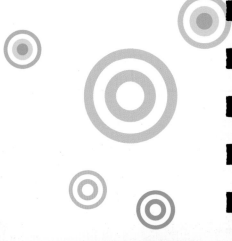